Love
Is a
Secret

Love
Is a
Secret

The Mystic Quest for Divine Love

by
Andrew Vidich

Aslan Publishing
310 Blue Ridge Drive
Boulder Creek, CA 95006
(408) 338-7504

Published by

Aslan Publishing
310 Blue Ridge Drive
Boulder Creek, CA 95006
(408) 338-7504

Vidich, Andrew, 1953-
  Love is a secret: the mystic quest for divine love / by Andrew
Vidich. — 1st ed.
     p. cm.
  Includes bibliographic references.
  ISBN 0-944031-04-8 : $16.95. — ISBN 0-944031-03-X (pbk.) : $9.95
  1. Mysticism. 2. love—Religious aspects. I. Title.
BL625.V46 1990
291.4'22—dc20
                                                                89-77328
                                                                     CIP

The photographs on pages 6, 48, 84, 92, 118, 126 and 136 were supplied by
Art Resource, New York and Giraudon Photography, Paris. Photos from the
Metropolitan Museum of Art, New York, on pages 38 and 140 are from the Fletcher Fund,
1963 and 1945 respectively; on pages 20 and 108 from a gift of Alexander Smith Cochran, 1913; on page
100 from the Rogers Fund and the Kevorkian Foundation Gift, 1955; on page 74 from a gift of
Edward C. Moore, Jr., 1928; and on page 64 from a gift of Jeffrey Paley, 1975.

Cover design by Brenda Plowman
Cover photo copyright The Image Bank
Printed in the USA
First Edition

10 9 8 7 6 5 4 3 2 1

Dedicated to all illuminated beings
who have graced this earth,
And my own Masters
Sant Kirpal Singh and Sant Darshan Singh
Who poured out in limitless measure
the true wine of God's love
on this unworthy soul.

Acknowledgements

I would like to acknowledge the help and inspiration of a number of people in the preparation of this book.

Thanks to Sandy English for typing the early drafts, to Art Stein for general comments, to my brother and mother for their review of the manuscript in the earlier stages, to Dawson Church for his general good council and excellent editing, and to Brenda Plowman for her design of the cover. Thanks too to Ruth Raziel, who commented on much of the material, to Barbara Carey and Tana Santa Cruz who typed later versions, and to Donna Ryan for her superb copyediting.

I would finally like to thank Tamir my wife for her excellent criticism and editorial assistance.

All of these people and many others helped make this book a reality and without their help this book would never have seen the light of day.

I would also like to acknowledge my spiritual Masters, Sant Kirpal Singh and Sant Darshan Singh. Kirpal Singh (1894-1974) of Delhi, India, began an intense search for a true spiritual Master at an early age. For years he investigated the claims of yogis and saints representing many schools of thought. His search culminated in initiation by Baba Sawan Singh of Beas. For twenty-four years he studied under his Master's guidance, and was chosen to succeed him in the spiritual line. Thereafter, he served as a spiritual Master, initiating over 120,000 disciples throughout the world and authoring over twenty books.

In 1974 he appointed Darshan Singh as his spiritual successor. Sant Darshan founded the Science of Spirituality organization, which now has over 550 centers. He was the author of several books of poetry, twice receiving the Urdu Academy award. In 1987 he appointed Sant Rajinder Singh as his spiritual successor, and passed from this world in 1989. Sant Rajinder may be reached at Kirpal Ashram, 2 Canal Rd., Vijay Nagar, Delhi 110009, India.

Contents

Preface

It has been a joy to work on, and now to offer to you, my research into the mystical experience of divine love, as described by the mystics from various religions and spiritual traditions. However, this book—though well documented—is not intended as an exercise in academic research.

The journey we take is anything but theoretical. It embodies the fullest expression of human capacity and potential, and embraces experiences that can only be described as supra-personal or supra-conscious. Wherever possible, these experiences are described in the mystics' own words.

The preparatory work for writing this book involved several difficulties. I read innumerable texts to find passages that were suitable. Many mystical treatises were not available in English translation. Also, out of hundreds of texts available, only a handful deal directly with the actual experience of the mystic, around which this book revolves.

Most important, the experience of the mystic needs special attention and differs from a conventional, or ordinary, perspective. Unlike Western psychologies, which are more or less understandable to the average person, mystic psychology describes levels of transcendent experience that are virtually impossible to compare with commonly understood modes of behavior. It is often extremely difficult to clearly define and articulate in ordinary language the experience of the mystic. Since language is but a feeble means of communication, I caution the reader not to mistake the moon for the finger that points to it.

This book is about the experience of divine love in the context of the lover-Beloved relationship. It does not attempt to be absolutely universal in application, because there are valid distinctions between spiritual disciplines. Nevertheless, I have made a conscious effort to show the uncanny similarity in experience between one religion and another.

This was easier with religions that are predisposed to a devotional—or to use the Indian term, "Bhakti"—approach to the divine. Despite obvious differences between the outer forms of worship practiced, the central core of the mystic's experience in devotional faiths, such as Islam, Christianity, Hinduism, Jainism, and Judaism, is essentially the same.

Buddhism and Taoism are considered exceptions by many theologians. Yet as different as their ideas may at first appear, their devotional essences are strikingly similar. Scholars who have pointed out lines of comparison include Angelus Silesius, the early sixteenth century Christian mystic, Thomas Merton, and the twentieth century Japanese mystic and scholar Toshihito Izutsu.

The immediate purpose of this book is to provide a map of the metaphysical psychology of this extraordinary relationship between the lover—the one approaching God—and God, the Divine Beloved, from its beginnings to its final consummation in union. Several distinct states of consciousness seem common across religious boundaries.

Some spiritual traditions might argue that all of these stages of attraction are illusory to begin with, for the entire outer world is illusory. From this perspective, the task of defining these transformations is merely labeling different aspects of illusion—clearly a meaningless task. While I admit the ultimate ontological reality of this argument, such a statement can have meaning only if spoken by those who are themselves free from the bondage of illusion. It is very much like trying to lecture a starving man that his experience of hunger is an illusion and he should not waste his time searching for food, as the body is just another form of deception.

The issue, and the focus of this book, is the real—indeed sometimes brutally real—experience of spiritual transformation. If this book does nothing else, it will surely eradicate the notion that the transformation of consciousness is child's play. As Kabir, the great fifteenth century Sufi teacher said, "When the arrow of separation hits, there's no healing; sobbing and sobbing you live dying and rise groaning."

It will be interesting for the reader to note that although the mystic's journey has as its goal eternal peace and bliss, much of the way is filled with agony and torture. Even the later stages of the path are rooted in the experience of duality—separation between lover and beloved—and are therefore often painful.

The supra-personal nature of this experience often defies description or analysis, not only because of the failure of language, but also because the experience transcends our cognitive and rational faculties. For this reason, mystics often speak in terms of symbol and metaphor. But even metaphor carries a profound power when uttered by one who has actually experienced this transformation. And this power is of immense value to others who are traveling along the same path. The mystics may make us laugh, cry, dance, or sing, but whatever we feel, we are moved to a deeper level of understanding by their utterances. Sant Kirpal Singh, a great twentieth- century mystic, used to say that the saints' words were always pregnant with meaning.

This book will be of inspiration and value only to those who have some interest in the spiritual path. It may have some value academically or theoretically, but that is a by-product and not the primary purpose. Rumi wrote, "My verses are like bread which is unleavened but by reading which the yeast of thought is applied; and by night they rise, and in the morning the bread of realization is found." In a similar way this book provides the raw "bread" upon which each of us must add the yeast of practice and contemplation.

Although this book looks at the experience of these stages of transformation in linear perspective, progressing in time from one state to another, not everyone experiences every aspect of the journey in the order given. In practice, progress may be fast or slow, direct or indirect, depending upon the perseverance, patience, steadfastness, and constitution of the lover. Nevertheless, amid all these varying conditions, an inner map emerges from which others may find guidance. And although we can identify ten stages through which the lover passes, it is extremely difficult in the later stages to distinguish among them.

In many cases, as Meher Baba has noted, the "God-communed" or "God-absorbed" lover may have little or no awareness of his or her station. But enough mystics and saints of all traditions have written of their experiences to give an insight into the stages that characterize spiritual transformation.

I am indebted to a number of people for their valuable assistance in preparing this manuscript; however, the guidance and spiritual inspiration of Sant Darshan Singh deserves more than special mention. His guidance has been invaluable; without it this book would never have seen the light of day. He provided the initial structure and content of the following chapters.

In 1977, I informally presented the project to him for his guidance and approval at his small government flat in Delhi. He began by remonstrating with me for my overzealous and irresponsible literary efforts. Sarcastically, yet humorously he pointed out the many errors and mistakes in my presumptuous attempt. Needless to say, I felt, as the saying goes, "nose deep in the waters of repentance." By the time the rebuke had ended, I realized that the task was well out of the range of my feeble experience and talent. Then he closed his eyes, which all the while had been focused intently on me, and went into a deep silence. After about ten minutes he opened them and, while steadily gazing at me, gave out in uncanny detail the plan and purpose of the book, chapter by chapter. When he was finished, he remarked that the words he had just uttered were the thoughts and exact instructions of Sant Kirpal Singh, who had left the earth plane three years previously. I left the room utterly humiliated—yet intoxicated with unimaginable bliss and joy.

When I returned to my room that evening, I realized it was no longer I who would complete this book, as I was clearly incapable, but the Master himself. As I have since seen, this has been entirely true at every step of this book's progress. He compiled and completed it long before I ever imagined it. As with most things in the field of spirituality, the greatest lesson seems to be humility first, humility second, and humility third.

Any failures and lapses are entirely a product of my pen. I can only hope that readers will find the mystics' words as priceless a jewel as I have found them to be and, understanding their true import, translate them into an enduring reality in their own lives. We may have filled libraries with the words of these great teachers, but if we have failed to integrate them into our lives, we bring ourselves no closer to true love and joy than before.

As Sant Darshan Singh has so aptly said, "The acid test of all spirituality is the degree to which we live it." This, in a few words, is the message of the life of every great teacher—and of our own.

Following page:
Christ on the Tree of Life
Academia, Florence

Originally executed for the Convent of Santa Clara in Florence in the early fourteenth century by Pacino da Bonaguido, this painting illustrates a religious text, the Lignum Vitae, by Saint Bonaventure. In the text he traces the origin of the Passion and Glorification of Christ in twelve chapters. In this painting they are represented as the twelve branches of a tree. At the top of the picture is Christ in Glory with the Madonna, and below them angels and saints. At the top of the Cross, between the prophets Daniel and Ezekiel, sits a pelican, traditional symbol of Christ's sacrifice. At the bottom of the picture are eight scenes from Genesis; above these on the left appear Moses and Saint Francis, and on the right Saint John and Saint Claire.

INTRODUCTION

Whether it is Shakespeare's *Romeo and Juliet,* the Psalms of David, or Wagner's *Tristan und Isolde,* themes of love permeate our entire culture. The universal language of love transcends all the limitations of speech, culture, religion, and concept that separate human beings. It is hard to find a single life that is not touched in some way by love.

As we look at love, we see innumerable ways in which it finds expression. We are familiar with familial love, romantic love, platonic love, and brotherly or sisterly love. Human artistic expression bears testimony to the depth of our acquaintance with these various expressions of love.

However, there is an expression of love which humanity as a whole has yet to understand and experience fully, and that is divine love. Although many have had some initial glimpses of this unique experience of love, humanity at large is still in its infancy in this respect. More often than not we confuse the ecstatic experiences of divine love with outer forms of worship or, worse, with religious fanaticism. The unfortunate result of this confusion is religious intolerance and a loss of faith in the validity and existence of the mystical experience.

Despite these cultural hurdles, in recent years the experience of divine love has become familiar to a growing number of people. In a recent *New York Times* poll, over 30 percent of all Americans indicated that they have had a transcendent or revelatory experience. In past societies, this transcendent experience was often thought to be the exclusive province of a select priestly or noble class. And our modern Western society has tended to treat mystical experiences with extreme skepticism and disapproval, as though they were a pathological deviation from normal human behavior. For their part, orthodox religions have treated reports of personal revelation with critical regard, if not outright hostility. Yet in the face of rampant materialism, religious intolerance, and violence on a global scale, large numbers of people are awakening to the the importance of spiritual rebirth.

Human and Divine Love

Through such personal experiences of illumination, we glimpse the experience of divine love. From the perspective of the mystic, all forms of love, whether divine or mundane, have as their base the same essence: the spontaneous attraction between two objects or beings, which finds its resolution in union.[1]

A great saint once remarked, "Love must love and a lover must have a beloved." Without an object of attraction, love remains dormant and latent. Whether that object is an attractive man or woman, a friend, or God, love must have a point of magnetism. We might assume that the mystic considers divine love the only valid form of love. Nothing could be further from the truth. The mystic emphatically states that all love, at whatever level, is a reflection of God's being.

In the East as well as in the West, a "spiritual love" is understood to exist when both lover and beloved transcend the limitations of merely physical or personal satisfaction in order to reach a state of spiritual oneness. This idea of love is a traditional symbol of the mystic's relationship to God.

The Original Love Myth

In the West, the original myth to explore romantic love in all its pathos was the epic tale of Tristan and Isolde. It was the first story in Western literature that dealt with romantic love. Robert Johnson suggests it is the source "of all our romantic literature from *Romeo and Juliet* down to the love story in the movie in the local cinema."[2]

Like all great myths, the story of Tristan and Isolde has the power to uplift us. It pulls us out of our petty and limited lives and into a grander and fuller vision of reality. Unlike many other great myths of both the East and the West, the myth of Tristan and Isolde is a profound expression of our Western psyche. This makes it a good introduction to the psychology of the mystic and his or her relationship to the Divine Beloved.

The troubadours were poets and musicians, often of knightly rank, who were most active between the eleventh and thirteenth centuries in France and Italy. If we look at their enduring tradition, we see expressed, perhaps for the first time, a way of love that seeks not only a physical union with the Beloved, but also a spiritual one. The lover is willing to forsake the physical relationship for a greater spiritual love. In Tristan's day, it was commonly believed that the world of the soul was to be gained, literally and symbolically, by sacrificing the desires of flesh. Terrible sufferings, anguish, and pain were all viewed as part of the transformative journey. What was this journey? It was the journey of the soul through the vale of tears. The unmitigated despair and suffering of the protagonists in romantic tales of that era was made bearable by the beauty, happiness, and perfection of the world into which they expected to enter.

Suffering, Death, and Transfiguration

The Cathars, an ascetic Christian sect contemporary with the troubadours, shared their belief that the path to the Divine Beloved necessitated suffering. They and the troubadours flatly stated that they were seeking entrance to the inner worlds through their passionate love. In most instances, they hoped to achieve spiritual beatitude by their physical death, because it released them from the slavery of the flesh. Passion, whether for a human or a Divine Beloved, gave them a foretaste of the ecstasy and yearning of the world to come. Romantic love was for them an initiation, a stepping stone to a higher, more glorious vision. In this respect their view of courtly human love paralleled the medieval view of spirituality. The inner worlds could be attained only through suffering, the ecstasy of their passion, or death.

If we look into the true meaning of the word *romantic*, we find that, epistemologically, it means one who has empathy or respect for the inwardness of others. It was precisely this inwardness with which the romantic lover strove to identify; when he was successful, he did indeed achieve a state of transcendence of himself and his limited world. The woman he loved was idealized into the symbol of all beauty and perfection and, indeed, in later centuries, was worshiped as Eros herself. Through Eros, goddess of love and symbol of perfect beauty, the lover was transfigured and transformed into the image of the beloved.

The whole tradition of romantic love, though greatly different today, has its grounding in the love and suffering of Tristan and Isolde. Today we fail to see our search for human love in this noble context, and yet all of us long for the perfect relationship that will fulfill us completely. Robert Johnson suggests that we are all on this quest, whether we see it consciously or whether it remains an unconscious archetype directing our lives.

Every culture has created its own mythologies around love. The quest for the Divine or Supreme Beloved is the great symbol, the great metaphor for the awakening of the soul. It is hard to find anyone who is not seeking this relationship in some way or another. The difference between the mystic and the early troubadours is that the mystic chooses a beloved who is the very personification of God; the incarnation of formless perfection. Saint John tells us that "The Word was made flesh and dwelt among us" (John 1: 1–5).

The early troubadours did the same thing by personalizing, in the form of their cherished lover, the ultimate, perfect ideal of the beloved. This symbol of the perfection of their love ignored the temporal and spiritual shortcomings of the actual person. Yet the personal sufferings of the mystic and the troubadour are strikingly similar. They represent the pain of every mortal who tries to give birth to the highest potentials within oneself. De Rougemont speaks of the psychology of romantic love when he asks us:

> *Why is it that we delight most of all in some tale of impossible love? Because we long for the branding; because we long to grow aware of what is on fire inside of us. Suffering and understanding are deeply connected; death and self-awareness are in league; and the European romanticism may be compared to a man to whom sufferings, and especially the suffering of love, are a privileged mode of understanding.*[3]

For us in the modern world, the path to higher awareness is no different than it was for the mystic of two thousand years ago or the troubadours of eight hundred years ago. The price for perfection is always the same, and that is suffering, trial and tribulation. The difference for us today is that most of us have failed to initiate this quest for our highest potential consciously. Rather, it is initiated for us by our latent unconscious needs for completion and lasting happiness. But instead of projecting all our ideals of perfection onto our husband or wife or lover who in the end can never fulfill those demands, we can instead turn within ourselves, to the Divine Beloved who can indeed fulfill these innate needs.

In the West, we are used to "falling in love." This initial attraction is so strong precisely because it reminds us of an ideal of perfection. In time, realizing the impossibility of this ideal in the shortcomings of our partner, we become bitterly disappointed. As Robert Johnson so artfully puts it, we "follow our projections about always searching for the one who will match the impossible ideal and will magically give us transformation."[4] When we don't find the divine world in our loved one, we suffer and fall into despair.[5]

When Saint Exupéry said, "Love is not so much looking into each other's eyes as it is looking in the same direction," he summarized the whole paradigm of the mystic. "For the mystic love is not something one falls into or out of. By its very nature such a thing would be impossible. For the mystic, love is about service." The great fifteenth-century teacher and poet Kabir said, "Love is giving, giving, and still more giving."

When Dr. Mohammed IqBal, poet laureate of India, was asked the meaning of the word "love" in his verses, he replied, "Love is the name for the continuous struggle, and there are many tests of love yet to be experienced beyond the stars and the sun."[6] For the lover of the Divine Beloved, love is a continuous restlessness of the heart. It is a constant yearning for greater perfection and greater selflessness.

The Bridge between Inner and Outer

The true lover is unaware, ironically, of the love that flows *through* him or her. Such a lover's life is shaped by the needs and hopes of others. For him or her, all creation is revealed to be the very image of the Beloved and therefore the closer he or she approaches the Beloved, the more ardent the desire to give of himself or herself selflessly. What this implies is that for the divine lover, every act must reflect the love in which he or she lives and moves.

For the lover who has bestowed his or her affection upon a competent spiritual teacher or guide, the very first place in which the process of transformation must occur is in the home, among those closest to one. The spark of love given by such a teacher first manifests itself as the love of parents, spouse, and community and is in fact what makes divine love a possibility.

One Sufi poet said, "the phenomenal is the bridge to the real." Without the phenomenal world, the real world can never be approached. The mystics' message throughout the ages has been a call to awaken to the deepest levels of love within ourselves. When love is awakened within our inner being, our perception of the universe undergoes a vast change. From this new vantage point, the mystic sees everything as endowed with love. Even the stars, sun, and moon are seen to move and orbit out of love. Mystics have stated that love is not only the driving energy behind all creation but the purpose for its existence. It is the force within humankind that has sought unity with God since the dawn of creation.

Mystics maintain that, since we are creations of God, and God's essence is love, it is in our very nature to love. Sant Kirpal Singh remarked, "Love is innate in our souls; we need only awaken it." Thus, if there is a difference between divine love and the love of human beings for each other, it is not in nature but in degree. Human love contains an element of selfishness in it. Divine love, in its purest form, it totally self-less. Divine love embodies a state of self-transcendence in which every trace of the self is completely removed.

Consider the example of a father who loves his son. He cares for his son, gives him the best education, clothing, and financial support, but does so with the idea that his son will one day become successful and help him in his old age. If the son does not succeed, the father becomes disappointed, and loses interest in his son. His love was tainted by selfish motives and hence falls short of being totally selfless. This love might better be termed love mixed with ego or desire.

Yet another kind of love is the love between a mother and her child. In this case, we have a mother who devotes her entire life to her child, giving up everything for her child's best interest. Even if the child does not live up to her expectations, she still goes on loving the child, caring for the child's welfare and giving more and more of herself. However, if the mother were to see a similar child on the street, one who is uncared for, unwanted, and destitute, she might not respond with the same love she gives own child. This shows that her love is limited to her child, the source of her personal interest and pleasure. Her love is a love colored by an aspect of selfish motivation.

Divine love, however, lies far beyond the scope of our personal self, for it seeks nothing for itself. It is a love that is totally self-giving and not self-seeking. Sant Darshan Singh has suggested that divine love "has only a beginning; it has no end." Viewed from this angle, divine love is characterized by a total absence of self; it is a love in which the lover is totally replaced by the Beloved. It is a love that has no existence outside of the Beloved and no individual will of its own. It is a love devoid of ego, which embraces the entire cosmos from atom to starry welkin.

The Ten Stages of Love

This book is organized around ten stages of divine love; distinct psychological states that characterize the mystic's journey. These stages first came into existence at the dawn of time but have rarely been articulated in modern times.

Chapter One introduces the concept of God as the ultimate source of love, whether human or divine, and man as the perfect image of His attributes. God, in His absolute state, exists as pure love; but in order to experience Himself, He projects Himself out as creation, or as the Holy Qur'an puts it, "From one He wished to become many" (Surah 2: 117).

Inherent in this outward projection was the simultaneous attraction of the soul to return to its original source.[7] In order to facilitate this process of return, God manifests Himself in the form of a God-personified being, who is the very reflection and perfection of all God's attributes and qualities. Such beings have been called by various names in different scriptures. Among the better-known ones are Christ, the Messiah, the Buddha, Guru, Murshid-i-Kamil, and Master. It is this God-man, or *rasul* (which literally means "mediator"), as the Sufis have called Him, who mediates and arranges for the return of the soul to its condition before the "envelopment in mind and matter." The perfect love of the God-man, who is himself a perfect reflection of God's love, awakens in the would-be lover a longing to return to his or her original condition of perfect peace and union.

The Master first attracts the heart of the lover by showering him or her with ecstasy-producing glances. These glances, being filled with the love of God, inebriate the lover and draw him or her gradually "into the lap" of the God-man. Once enamored of the Master, he or she becomes absorbed in the loving remembrance of the Divine Beloved. This stage has sometimes been referred to in mystic terminology as becoming "lost in the tresses of the beloved."

William Butler Yeats, in his poem *Sailing to Byzantium*, describes this unique attraction of the soul to the inner Master:

O Sages standing in God's holy fire
As in the gold mosaic of a wall,
Come from the Holy fire, perne in a gyre,
And be the singing-masters of my soul.

Consume my heart away; sick with desire
And fastened to a dying animal
It knows not what it is; and gather me
Into the artifice of eternity.

As the lover's yearning for the beloved increases, the experience of separation becomes so painful that death itself appears desirable. Abdullah Muhammed, who depicts the agonizing plight of a woman caught in the pangs of separation from God, once said, "The yearning for the Divine Beloved is consuming me. I am tired of this life and wish to purchase death in the marketplace."

In succeeding chapters we explore the relationship between divine love and lust, and the gradual abandonment of the latter in favor of the former. "Lust" is here taken to mean not only physical love but all the pleasures of the senses. When individual consciousness attaches itself to its source, which is God, divine love results. Conversely, when human consciousness is attached to material enjoyments, it is wrapped up in lust or egotistic desire.

The Final Stage: Oneness

In the last few of these ten stages, we see the lover gradually becoming completely lost in a state of intoxication. At this point the lover, having tasted the divine nectar of love, is unable to leave it. Ibin-Farid, a Sufi poet and mystic of the thirteenth century, aptly describes this wine, which intoxicates the lover: "If a lover of God watered the earth of a tomb with the divine wine, the dead one would recover his soul and his body revive."[8] The effect of this "wine" cannot be fully described in words, for it is an experience with no earthly equivalent.

In the Bible, the *Song of Songs* very clearly refers to this: "I am drunk with wine and filled with bliss."[9] Not only is this divine wine a source of permanent peace and inebriation for the lover, but it lifts the lover out of his or her state of rational and logical understanding. Plato said, "The madness that comes of God is superior to the sanity which is of human origin."[10] This state of madness that results from inner intoxication by spiritual wine is not illogical but supra-logical. The "wisdom of the world is foolishness with God" (I Cor. 3:19).

This seeming madness, or more truly mindlessness, shatters the veils of phenomenal existence and must perforce appear to the world as insanity. Jalaluddin Rumi expresses this divine yearning of the lover eloquently: "It behooves us to become ignorant of this worldly wisdom: rather we must clutch at madness."[11]

It is this mindlessness which is the root of the tree of wisdom and prophecy. John Smith, the Platonist, acknowledged this state when he said, "There must be some kind of *mavia* [madness] in all this prophecy."[12]

In the final stages of awakening, we see the lover seasoned to live in a state of longing, pain, and anguish. When this torment paradoxically starts becoming a relief from his pain, the lover begins to merge into the Beloved and ultimately becomes one with Him. Ghalib, the Indian Urdu poet, has tried to render this inexplicable state in words:

> *When your sorrows exceed all limits,*
> *You become accustomed to those sorrows,*
> *And once you become accustomed to those sorrows,*
> *They become a part of your life.*

Gradually, a turning point comes when the lover loses all self-identity and merges completely in the Beloved. When this stage is reached, the lover may look into the mirror, but finds only the image of the Beloved there, not his or her own image. Mystic literature is replete with stories and anecdotes of this often-misunderstood state. Allegory or metaphor is used to describe a condition that cannot be adequately conveyed by ordinary language.

The greatest romance in classic Persian literature is that of Leila and Majnun. In this epic, we find an excellent example of the use of metaphor for the spiritual journey itself. As it is told, after a long and torturous periods of separation in which Majnun has quite literally wasted away in the desert awaiting his beloved Leila, she returns to be reunited with him. To her dismay, she can no longer recognize him. His sufferings have reduced him to less than a skeleton, more ghost than human.

As she listens closely, she hears an unfamiliar voice repeating her name, coming from a tree. She looks more closely, and a strange, emaciated figure emerges from the base of the trunk. She cries out, "I am myself, Leila, and who are you?" Hearing these words, Majnun goes into a state of shock and says, "If you are Leila, then who am I?" His longing has led him to identify totally with his Beloved. After uttering these words, he gives an anguished shriek and dies.

When love reaches such climaxes, the lover forgets his own identity. Love then is beyond the reckoning of the rational mind; only experience will capture it. At this point it is not love that resides in the heart of the lover. The Beloved Himself has taken up residence. At this divine banquet, lover and Beloved unite, mystery after mystery is laid open, and the dualism of object and subject, of knower and known, ceases. Only the full beatitude of love remains. This experience is neither exterior nor interior, but wholly present simultaneously. Saint Bonaventure (*Mentis*, 5) explains this paradox by saying:

> *God's center is everywhere.*
> *His circumference nowhere.*

Sant Darshan Singh, in poetic verse, referred to this universal center:

> *We must become all eyes like the narcissus*
> *and once having become all eyes,*
> *we will see the beloved in every eye.*[13]

From this "eye of eternity" all of us are being called by love. And it is this call that is heard again and again in the heart of the lover. Farid-ud-din Attar, a poet and mystic saint of India, echoes this call which is the basis for our very existence:

> *In love no longer "Thou" and "I" exist.*
> *For self has passed away in the beloved.*
> *Now will I draw aside the veil from Love,*
> *And in the temple of mine inmost soul*
> *Behold the Friend, Incomparable Love.*
> *He who would know the secret of both the worlds,*
> *Will find the secret of them both is Love.*[14]

Following page:
Leila and Majnun in the Desert
Metropolitan Museum of Art, New York

In this beautiful depiction of the love story of Leila and Majnun from the Khamseh of Nizami (Mirror of the Invisible World), Majnun meets Leila in the desert after a period of the most intense agony and separation. Here Majnun is reduced to a ghost of a skeleton while singing his heartrending songs to Leila. The two lovers gaze upon each other with joy and wonder, as they had when they were children. For the mystic, this story illustrates the fire of separation, which consumes everything, including the lover's body and soul in desperate longing, as well as the supernal joys of union.

CHAPTER 1

Universal Man:
Stages in the Unfoldment of Love

In every scripture, whether of the East or the West, the human being is represented as the microcosmic symbol of the metacosmic being. All states of consciousness, from the atom to the absolute, are contained in and latent in the form of man. The human soul comprises within itself all possibilities as well as all forms of manifest existence, from the humblest rock to the greatest prophet.

The human being, according to Sufi belief, is the symbol of universal existence, the most perfect manifestation of God on earth, the prototype of God in human form.

Different traditions have variously decribed this prototype as the Perfect Man or *al-Insanu-al-Kamil* (Sufis) *Adam Qadmon* (Kabbala) and *Chun Jen* or *Wang* (Taoism). All exemplify the being that has fully realized the richness of all of life and the sum total of all possibilities latent in Being itself. The perfect expression of these potentialities is a gift of pure love, translated by God's love into the created world of forms.[1]

This manifestation of perfect love in the being of the Perfect Man is the first gift of love absolute. The primordial Adam is none other than the first spark of love to descend into the world of time, the "I Am That I Am" from which all souls originate. Meister Eckhart, the thirteenth-century Christian mystic, affirms this truth when he writes:

When the soul strips off her created nature
there flashed out its uncreated prototype.[2]

Paradoxically, then, the soul's return to God is a return to itself, for all souls actually pre-existed in God. Al-Hallaj was a tenth-century saint put to death for his beliefs. He is sometimes known as the martyr of love. During a moment of spiritual elevation, he expressed this truth:

I saw my Lord with the eye of the heart, And I said, "Who are you?" He answered, "You."[3]

"To see the world in a grain of sand and eternity in a flower" is not just the work of the poet; it is the vision of the mystic. For the mystic, the inward is actually the outward, the real. The *Zohar*, the book of Jewish mystical teaching, says:

God made this terrestrial world in the image of the world above; thus all which is found above has its analogy below...and everything constitutes a unity.[4]

Mystics from all cultures and times have alluded to the divine imprint in manifestation and pointed out that every creation, however small, corresponds to a higher celestial ideal. For the mystic, all things are teachers. There are "books in rivulets and sermons in stones" for those who see the divine correspondences. In the Kaula Tantra, it is said, "From Brahman to a blade of grass all things are my gurus."

We human beings stand in a unique place in our similitude to the Creator. We are like a glass that is both translucent and transparent, radiating and reflecting simultaneously the perfect light and love of the Creator. In the Bible this correspondence is alluded to in a number of places but most clearly in the Old Testament, when it states, "Man is made in the image of God."

Love: The Perfect Path

The human being is, in brief, the microcosm of the entire universe who participates in the infinite qualities and being of God to the extent that he or she realizes that potential. This innate affinity with God is expressed and embodied most clearly in the essence and manifestation of love. The divine correspondences are most perfectly realized in and through the medium of love, because our essence is love.

The call to love is a call already latent within us as love. Sant Kirpal Singh confirms this truth when he states that since our own essence is identical to God's, and since God's essence is love, the most perfect method of return to God is love as well. The path, then, can only be one of love, for:

> *There is no goal beyond love, because love is both the beginning and the end of the path. In this way, God's love and our own are identical, for one who has divine love has reached God.*[5]

The poet and saint Misbah-ul-Hayut spoke of this identity of the Divine Beloved with the lover as well:

> *The Almighty loved Himself if ye should know,*
> *Made the universe His own mirror to see Himself aright*
> *Displayed His beauty to Himself,*
> *Really He is the lover, Beloved and love itself.*[6]

The movement of the separate ray of the soul back to its primal and original source—God—is a journey through the veils of ego and limitation to selflessness and infinite power. An individual's spiritual unfoldment is marked by a number of stages and states associated with acquiring the attribute of love. There are many ways in which love can be made manifest in the outer world. In a similar way, spiritual love takes many different forms and expressions.

In the Hindu Bhakti tradition there are essentially four degrees of spiritual relatedness which the disciple must traverse in order to attain the highest perfection of spiritual union. The Bhakti sage Shrivatsa Goswami explains that a disciple first has the relationship to Krishna as master (dasya). This gives way to filial respect (vatsalya), then to deep, intimate friendship (sakhya), and finally to the lover-Beloved relationship (madhurya), and the total realization of the Beloved (rasa). This progression, catalyzed by worldly circumstances, involves a gradual increase in devotion, faith, and direct experience of the Beloved. In the final stage, the soul relates to God as a Beloved, and the progression thereafter is in that lover-Beloved relationship.[7]

The Sacred Marriage

All souls are in fact female in relationship to God, for it is in our capacity to receive—to be emptied of everything—that we move into the divine embrace with the Divine Beloved.

In the Christian tradition, we have innumerable examples corroborating this point. The church, or communion of the faithful, is referred to in the New Testament as the "bride of Christ." Cardinal Newman also used the analogy of a wedding to describe the individual's connection with God:

If a man wants the full bliss of contact with God,
let him behave as a wife.

Saint John of the Cross prayed,

O my God, make me Thy wedded wife;
Unless You take me in Your embrace,
I can have no peace, no bliss.

When Saint Francis of Assisi saw the astral, or light, form of Christ, he called out, "Oh my dear husband, You have wedded me." Finally, we have the unambiguous words of Saint Catherine,

I have been betrothed to Christ, and He has given me a ring to wear. This He has given as the sign of His love.[8]

In the Sufi tradition, love in its mature state is always depicted as longing for the Divine Beloved. Jami, a fifteenth-century Sufi master and poet, cries out for the Beloved of his soul in tones that render mortal cares insipid:

Better to catch one moment's glimpse of thee,
Than earthly beauties love through life retain.[9]

Or again, in the poetic revelry of Sheikh Ahmad al'Alawi:

Closer drew herself toward me,
Raised the cloak that hid her from me.
Made me marvel to distraction,
Bewildered me with all her beauty.
She took me and amazed me,
And hid me in her inmost self,
Until I thought that she was I,
And my life she took as ransom.[10]

Love in the temporal world, through whatever phenomena it is expressed, forms the foundation and support for the divine marriage that is consummated in the heart. This love is the perfect prototype for the lover's union with the Divine Beloved. Meister Eckhart draws us to this realization when he says, "As there is wedlock between a man and wife so there is wedlock between God and the soul."[11] Rumi, speaking of his ecstatic union with his beloved teacher Shamsi of Tabriz, to whom he addressed thousands of his poems, sums up the union of lover and Beloved when he says, "I do not wear a shirt when I sleep with the Adored One."

This sacred marriage, consummated in the bed of the heart, implies the deepest of mysteries. The divine marriage is tantamount to both our death and our resurrection. The word "marry" (*eko bhu* in Hindi) means "to become one," but also means "to die." This marriage implies our death, because until we have become consumed by the divine splendor, we cannot be fully at one with the Beloved.

Such a marriage implies resurrection as well, because in this death there is full identification with the eternal Beloved. In the path of love, the lover soon realizes that there is no room for duality. Consummation of the spiritual journey is attained when lover, Beloved and love are transformed into one essence. Abu Said ibn Abi 'L Khayr says:

Lover, Beloved and Love am I
Beauty and Mirror and the Eyes that see.[12]

The path of spiritual realization, viewed from the lover's perspective, is an alchemical process of transmuting the base soul of man, corrupted in the marketplace of form, into a "virgin" soul fit for the bed of God.

On the Way to the Wedding

Before any person becomes drawn to God, that person's thinking is predicated on a sense of separation between himself or herself and the Beloved. God is perceived as a distant being; some people—the lovers—are utterly discontent unless they are being drawn toward a state of union with this Being. The whole journey of love occurs in the consciousness of the lover. It starts with separation and ends with union.

The Emissary Society, a modern spiritual school founded on the esoteric principles of Christianity, uses a particular formula which encapsulates the milestones on this journey:

Radiation
Response
Attraction
Union
Unified Radiation

Radiation, in this context, means the radiance that emanates from the Divine Beloved, or God, or from a spiritual teacher. To the extent that any of us partake of the radiance of God, we are ourselves radiant. This divine radiation is powerfully attractive.

This radiance is initially supplied from outside to the person who is responsive to God, usually through a spiritual friend or teacher. When exposed to this radiance, the heart of the lover is kindled into *response*. Response involves an acknowledgment by the lover of kinship with the spirit of radiance, and a desire to move toward the expression of this.

This desire to draw closer is known as *attraction*. It draws the lover closer to the Beloved, and the power of radiance emanating from the Beloved has all kinds of specific effects on the lover. The closer the lover comes, the more his or her consciousness is transformed. This journey of attraction has many stages within it, which have been mapped by mystics and sages throughout the ages. We will draw on the wisdom of these great teachers extensively in pages of this book.

The consummation of the state of attraction is *union*, in which the lover ceases to exist as an entity separate from the Beloved; all personal desires and characteristics are lost as the lover joins without any reservation whatever with the Beloved.

At this point, lover and Beloved cease to exist as self-aware individuals; their awareness is completely centered in God, and they are both perfectly responsive instruments in His hand. This is the stage of *unified radiation.* Where at the beginning there was one perfectly realized being, the Beloved, there are now two, and the two join together in extending the blessings of the universe into the earth. Their outer capacities of body, mind, and heart are receptacles totally devoted to the expression of God's will, to being His agents on earth.

The path toward the state of unified radiation has a number of particular characteristics; sages from all ages and many cultures have mapped the road. The stations of love referred to below are their markers on the journey. Although there are many different religions and spiritual traditions, there is a remarkable similarity in the actual experience of the lover walking this road. It is a path that cuts across culture, creed, and time.

The Stations of Love

In organizing this book around ten basic stages of divine love, I have drawn from the work of a number of great mystics and Masters of both the East and the West. Foremost among them are Khawaja Nasir-al-din, the Sufi sage of Delhi, Sant Darshan Singh and Sant Kirpal Singh, Meister Eckhart, Guru Nanak, Kabir, Shankara, Attar, Ahmad Ghazzali and contemporary Masters. It would be prudent to note here that the delineation of this journey into ten stations is not fixed in stone. Theoretically there may be many more stages of finer and finer degrees; however, these particular stations define certain universal aspects of the journey toward the gnosis that corroborate with other religious traditions. In addition what is critical here is the underlying change of consciousness that these stations represent.

It is important to remember that these stages are not intellectual concepts but spiritual states. They are therefore subjective descriptions of reality.

These states represent unique turning points or transformations. Each one poses certain immediate and direct challenges to the lover. Since each soul is unique, each one's responses will likewise contain different subjective elements. But in general they can be organized around the unifying principles of separation and union, and the dissolving of the lover's identity as a separate and distinct entity.

The Honeymoon of Divine Love

The first station of this remarkable journey of love is called the "call" by Christians. It is this period the lover experiences the initial pangs of longing for God. During this first phase the lover is put through a series of difficult trials and outer purifications in order to cleanse the lover of his or her wordly dross. This phase of preparatory cleansing is orchestrated by the Beloved in order to test the soul's depth of longing and sincerity. The Divine Beloved makes arrangement for the meeting of the Guru with the disciple. "When the disciple is ready," the saying goes, "the Guru appears."

This period is one in which the soul is often confused and filled with doubts. His or her heart is essentially still enmeshed in the world and its affairs and is easily sidetraced or diverted from its course.

This stage of the lover-Beloved relationship is also characterized by an overwhelming display of personalized love for the person concerned, given by the beloved. This desire, in due course, intensifies to such an extent that the lover's uppermost desire is to be in the physical presence of the Beloved. The Beloved in turn responds by granting this desire in proportion to the lover's need, and receptivity to the Beloved.

In this initial contact, the Beloved often showers an overwhelming amount of personal affection upon the lover. The Beloved's glances give the lover a taste of the divine nectar of love. In this rare display of personalized love, the lover responds by drinking deeply of the love of the Beloved. This stage is consummated when the silken bonds of love are tied in the corridors of the heart and the lover's fate is sealed by a deep and abiding attachment to the Beloved.

During this phase, which some Buddhist Masters have called the honeymoon of love, the Beloved almost spoils the lover for good with his personal solicitude and communication. The love of the lover, however, remains entirely exteriorized, for it has yet to experience any sort of test of fidelity or sincerity. This phase is called *ulfa* by the Sufis and *rati* (attachment) by Kabir.

Internalizing the Process

The second station of love is primarily focused on testing the lover's sincerity and faith and interiorizing the process of love. In Sufi terminology, it has been called *sadaqa* (truth), because it is here that the lover's loyalty and commitment meet their first challenges. The lover, during this stage, often meets with intense criticism and rebuke from both friends and family. In some cases the lover finds himself or herself completely alone and abandoned.

In the second phase of this station, the helpless lover now encounters, to his or her immense surprise, cruel rebukes from the lips of the Beloved himself. The Beloved, in seeking to interiorize the lover's love, often hurls barbed arrows into the heart of the lover. The fortunate lover, however, realizes that this, too, is a gift from the Beloved and accepts these rebukes with humility and gratitude.

After undergoing many a rebuke and tribulation at the hands of the Beloved, the lover quickly learns to examine his or her heart and discover when he or she is in error. The completion of this stage is reached when the lover is able to swim in the ocean of the Beloved's love without the boat of personal attention.

The lover, having made a complete turnaround from the privileged state of intimacy, now nourishes his or her love through the inner remembrance of the Beloved. Within the Christian mystic tradition, this is described by Saint John of the Cross as the "kindling of the living flame of love" and represents the lover's ability to nourish his or her love *with or without* the Beloved's outer display of affection.

The Vale of Tears

In the third stage of this remarkable journey, the heart of the lover ripens with longing for the Beloved. The gradual increase of inner light produces in proportional measure a restlessness and agony that the lover has never known before. This agony cannot be contained in the fragile heart of the lover.

Being still raw in love, the lover bewails his or her lot and retreats into the darkest corners of sorrow and depression. Withdrawing into his or her heart still further, the lover begins to shed copious tears in desperation for the Beloved. These tears signal the beginning of a process of interiorizing the lover's love. This station is completed when the lover becomes caught in the manacle of the Beloved's glances and accepts without complaint a position of servitude and dependence.

The Valley of Separation

Movement into the fourth stage begins only after separation becomes unbearable and the predominant experience of the lover is profound agony coupled with a passionate and unceasing inner remembrance of the Beloved. This station is distinguished from the preceding one in several ways.

First, the lover remains in a state bordering on death. Death, in fact, appears to the lover to be the only release from this terrible torture. The lover spends his or her nights in prolonged vigils, sheds copious tears, and prays for death to overtake him or her. The lover eats little, talks little and in general severs his or her connection, with worldly pursuits. In passing through this valley of separation, the lover adds the glance of his or her own love *for* the Beloved to the glance of loveliness *from* the Beloved. In other words, the lover's longing and desperate need for the Beloved are facets of the Beloved's need for the lover's love.

The glance of the Beloved is, in Sufi terminology, called the *glance of loveliness*. It is a transforming experience for one who can receive the revelation it contains. However, it does not become the glance of belovedness until the lover is nullified while gazing into the eyes of the Beloved. The Beloved's beauty is contingent upon the recognition of that beauty by the lover. Otherwise his beauty remains in the realm of the imagination.

In this stage the lover quickly matures in his or her love and realizes not only the emptiness of his or her own being, but also the grandeur of the Beloved's beauty. So long as the lover is preoccupied with his or her own search, he or she does not taste of the tree of union. The lover's nullification of himself or herself is the first phase of this process of separation. It then proceeds through the corridors of endurance and proceeds to complete resignation.

This resignation on the part of the lover allows the Beloved to handle the whole affair as He likes. In giving up the tantalizing fruit of union, the lover realizes that the agony of separation itself, in the strangest of ways, is the cure for itself. The fire that once consumed him or her, he or she now consumes with relish. This is the point at which *the lover begins to merge with the Beloved.*

The heart of the lover becomes seasoned to living in a state of anguish and even begins to enjoy the "atrocities of the Beloved." Sant Darshan Singh observed:

Others are leading a life of goblets and cups of wine served to them, and are getting intoxicated with cup after cup. I derive my intoxication from the cold-blooded murder of my desires.[13]

The Feast of Inner Radiance

In the fifth stage of the journey, the lover enters the feast of inner radiance and subsists on the inner radiant form of the Beloved. This station has been called *shaqhif* by the Sufis, *illumination* by the Christians and *dhyana* by the Yogasutras. During this stage the lover is required to exhibit three distinct traits.

First, he or she spontaneously carries out the commands of the Beloved without intellectual questioning.

Second, he or she remains continuously alert against anything that may enter the tavern of his or her heart except God.

Third, the lover is required to maintain absolute secrecy with regard to his or her love for the Beloved.

During this stage, the lover lives on the inner radiant showers of light and love bestowed upon him or her from within the temple of the heart. The lover's days are filled with remembrance, and his or her nights are an endless round of vigils and fasts.

Turning from the Other

In the sixth station, which has been called *khulla*, or "exclusive attachment," by the Sufis, the lover turns from himself or herself, the world, and all things that are "other." This includes even the Beloved. As he or she breaks the idols of "otherness," the ecstatic vision of the Beloved enfolds within the lotus of his or her heart. In this stage the book of ecstasy is opened and the lover lives in certitude and trust. Every moment for the lover is a sacrifice, and he or she offers a thousand hearts with every passing moment.

The Palace of Unity

During the seventh station, the lover becomes unmoved by any outer disgrace, blame, poverty, or condition. The Beloved in turn responds by perfecting the lover's conduct in the world and opens up the book of creation to him. The lover steps into the palace of unity and becomes a person of true insight.

In this field of unity the lover's actions in the world of forms exhibit perfect serenity and he or she acts without the least bit of personal desire. The lover pays homage to the Divine Beloved, whom he or she now witnesses in every atom, in every leaf, and in every shining petal. Having reached the door of the Beloved, his or her ardor for complete and final union knows no limits. Standing and gazing at the glory of the Beloved, the lover unabashedly awaits his or her own extinction.

The Madness of Love

During the eighth station, called ecstasy or *wajud*, by the Sufis, the lover takes the plunge into the sea of intoxication and loses his or her reason and senses. During this precarious stage, the lover resembles a madman who runs hither and thither

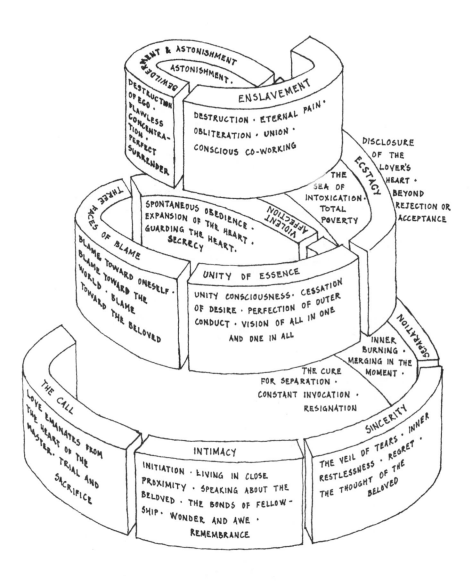

The above illustration depicts the ten stages of love as an upward spiral.
The primary characteristics of each state are shown.

wildly in search of the Beloved. Overwhelmed by this ocean of intoxication, the lover converses with the trees and the stones, in a wild rampage of love. Here the inner worlds illuminate his or her way and every cry for help is met by a thousand shafts of light. The lover's whole being has become a polished mirror reflecting and radiating the light of the Beloved's love. The great Sufi saint Al Yafi'i gives us a hint of this state when he says:

> *They say: Thou art become mad with love for thy Beloved. I reply: The savior of life is for madmen.*[1]

The Disappearance of Reality

The ninth station has been called "astonishment and bewilderment" by the Sufis and "death in Christ" by the Christians. In this stage the lover experiences the most brutal of sorrows and humiliations. The very ground upon which he or she walks appears to be a mirage, and the seven heavens and all the universes appear as dust before the supremacy of his or her love. The lover can find no resting place within or without.

Ironically, although he or she is encamped in the tavern of unity, the lover knows nothing of himself or herself, and weeps for a Beloved about whom he or she knows nothing. In this stage the lover experiences complete isolation from everything. There is not even the slightest thread of connection. In this state reality itself disappears, there is neither eternity nor noneternity, neither existence nor nonexistence. Here life has no meaning outside the "tresses of the Beloved." Al-Hallaj said:

> *I am he whom I love and he whom I love is I*
> *We are two spirits dwelling in one body*
> *If thou seeth me thou seeth Him,*
> *If thou seeth Him thou seeth us both.*[2]

Or in the words of Saint John, "It is not now I that liveth but Christ in me." The lover at this point is quite willing to stake his or her life on the Beloved. For there is no concern any longer for one's own life. Sant Darshan Singh spoke beautifully of this wondrous state :

Give me one glance of your love and I
Would be willing to suffer your
Cruelties for the rest of my life.[3]

Annihilation

The tenth and final stage enumerated by Chiragh-i-Delhi is that of death or annihilation. At this stage the lover is beset by tremendous dangers and obstacles. Here the full force of unthinkable suffering falls upon the head of the one who makes this journey. This state is characterized by total indifference on the part of the Beloved and total helplessness on the part of the lover. Ibn Arabi describes these final stages in his book *Journey to the Lord of Power.* Here the creed of the lover is only intoxication, and it is an intoxication that leads to eradication, then absence, then crushing, or the complete shattering forever of the ego and sense of reality of the lover.

This in turn leads to *fana,* or destruction, wherein the lover is totally annihilated and then lost even to annihilation. Here the lover exists only in name. To quote one great Sufi:

Love is the negation of all the attributes of the lover and the positioning of the Beloved Himself in their place.

Although each of these ten states is unique and poses a particular challenge or test, certain stages may appear to overlap or to take place simultaneously. One of the problems of presenting a book organized into such sections is that the description of each stage makes it seem somehow detached from the preceding and subsequent stage. For the lover, however, these experiences appear to flow fluidly from one stage to another, and sudden catalytic moments occur only rarely.

It is also important to note that the experience of these various states—of longing, trust, faith, certitude, ecstasy and so on—is present in all stages of the journey to one degree or another. The changes in stage are identified by the degree to which a particular state is experienced, and in the way it affects the lover's understanding of him- or herself.

Thus, there may be many moments of ecstasy during the journey, even in the initial stages, but these are not to be confused with the stage in which ecstasy is not a passing phase but the predominant inner dynamic of the lover's reality.

One example of this subtle difference is distinguishing between the states of *hal* and *maqum*. The great Rumi gives us a visual and poetic explanation:

> *The* hal *state is like the unveiling of that beauteous bride, while* maqum *station is the being alone with the bride.*[4]

Though at times these states are difficult to clearly articulate, their existence is an esoteric fact to those who have traveled the path of divine love. The Qur'an (Surah VI:75–79, verse 83) states:

> *We raise unto degrees of wisdom whom we will.*
> *Lo. Thy Lord is Wise, Omniscient.*

These descriptions are not meant to represent absolute reality; the actual experiences are too subtle. But they can certainly provide wayfarers with a taste of what is yet to come. Understanding the process can prepare the lover to recognize the challenge of the moment. Awareness of the significance of the moment is the precondition upon which appropriate response is built. If there is no awareness, the moment passes, and the perfection of the moment is lost.

Following page:
The Conference of the Birds
Metropolitan Museum of Art, New York

These miniatures are by a seventeenth-century Iranian artist,
Habib Allah. In the story of the Conference of the Birds by twelfth-
century Persian poet and mystic Attar, the hoopoe (left), the symbol of
inspiration (the guide), assembles the birds (faculties) to begin the
quest for the fabulous Simurgh (God). Those who are attached to the
sensory world give excuses for not making the journey. The nightingale,
or that aspect of the self caught in the exterior form of things, cannot
leave the rose: the duck cannot leave the water; the hawk cannot leave
its prey. Only those faculties (and souls) that have been awakened
from within to the inner aspect of reality choose to make the journey
towards completion. At the end the birds find that the Simurgh has
been with them all along, guiding them from within, throughout the
journey.

The Call:
Love Emanates from the
Heart of the Master

God became man, that man might become God.
—Saint Athanasius, Saint Augustine, Saint Cyril of Alexandria, Meister
Eckart, Jacob Boehme, Rumi, Kirpal Singh, Hafiz, Rama Krishna, Meher Baba,
Sai Baba, Christ...and many others.[1]

Almost all spiritual traditions have laid great stress on the
need for a guide or teacher on the spiritual journey. The very
first stage of the journey to God involves the lover in a direct
relationship with the guide or Master. Sant Kirpal Singh has
stated this quite forcefully:

*All great spiritual teachers have maintained that without
the help of a living Master the spiritual journey is a difficult
and impossible traverse to the very end.*[2]

Swami Ramdas (1886–1963) went so far as to say, "Even God
cannot grant *moksha* (deliverance) but only the guru." This
seeming overstatement is justified, for the spiritual guide or

rasul (intercessor) is the very means by which liberation is achieved.

Mysticism, then, begins with an invitation by the teacher, and the lover-Beloved relationship begins.

In the Christian scriptures John tells us, "You have not chosen me, but I have chosen you" (John 15:16). In Christian terms, it is Christ who first loves us. Our love is only reciprocal. John tells us again, "We are to love then, because He first loved us" (I John 4:19). It is the God-man, the guru, the Christ, who initiates our love for Him, without which there would be no relationship at all to begin with. It is through the God-man that the power of God acts and moves. Masters are living representatives of God. They have developed all the qualities of God. Though material, they are windows to the infinite.

The first stage of this relationship of the lover to Master or guide, begins when the lover feels the inner pull to live in close proximity to the Master. In mystic literature, love is always depicted as emanating from the heart of the Beloved. It is this love that first fires the lover into greater and greater attachment to the Master. During this stage the lover, moved by the grace apparent in the initial gift, seeks the door of a guide or Master.

In the Old Testament this point is alluded to in the book of Ecclesiastes (6:36):

If thou see a man of understanding,
go to him early in the morning
and let thy foot wear the steps of his doors.

In his initiation in the wilderness, Abraham was blessed by Melchizidek, king of Salem. There are similar examples throughout the Scriptures for the notion that without contact with a guide or Master, spirituality is unrealizable.

Some Masters have gone so far as to insist that those who are not under the guidance of a Master are under the guidance of Satan, the master of the material world. Bayazid al-Bistami, the great Sufi Master known for his miraculous powers, once said, "The guide of those who have no guide is Satan."[3] Jesus Christ said, "He who is not for me is against me." Jesus describes the role of the God-man in the simplest of language (Luke 10:22):

No man knoweth the Son, but the father;
Neither knoweth any man the Father, save the Son
And he to whosoever the Son will reveal him.

Sant Kirpal Singh simiarly supports this role of the God-man: "God is unchangeable and everlasting permanence. But we have not yet seen Him. So we have, of necessity, to bestow our loving devotion on the human pole where the Power-of-God is manifest." Guru Amardas Ji, the Third Guru of the Sikhs, says, "If you want to worship God, worship the Satguru, who is God personified or the Word made Flesh."[4]

The notion that spiritual practice can be successfully attempted without the aid of some Master soul is fraught with danger. Rumi reminds us in his poetic tongue,

The fleshly soul is a dragon
with hundred-fold strength and cunning:
the face of the Shaykh [Master]
is the emerald that plucks out its eye.[5]

Many wonderful words have been written about the greatness of the Master souls and the wondrous things that happen in their presence. Simply being in their company charges the disciple with profound spiritual uplift. Sant Kirpal Singh expresses this point very clearly:

Masters are the overflowing cups of the Lord's intoxicating
color—overflowing vessels of love. Just by enjoying His
company the yearning for God is born within one's being.
He creates love, for He is all love, He teaches how to love—
the rays of love issue forth from Him wherever He goes.
His words are uttered to increase the love within us.[6]

The entire edifice of love is predicated and built upon the relationship between the teacher and the disciple.

This profoundly important connection with the teacher is established initially through the gift of initiation. Moinuddin Chisti has stated that "Those beings who have reached that illuminated state of perfection have the ability to enlighten the hearts of the people with divine light."[7] Speaking of this priceless gift, Swami Sivananda, a modern Indian saint, described the process of initiation as the "direct link with the divine being."[8]

The Master as Expert

Although the tradition of the living Master has been customary in Sufi and Hindu Buddhist Traditions, there is ample evidence in Christianity, Judaism, and Taoism to support the need for a living guide capable of direct spiritual transmission. Thomas Norton, a renowned English alchemist of the fourteenth century, spoke of the Master or teacher as One divinely sent by God to instruct the disciple so that he or she may be taught from "mouth to mouth."[9] Chang Po-tuan, familiar with the secret oral teachings of Chinese alchemy, also warned against "constrained conjecture" and the inability to "succeed unless you have a true teacher."[10] In reality there is little or no difference between a realized Master and God Himself.

This realization, however, is hardly imaginable during the beginnings of this relationship. A novice can seldom recognize a true Master, even if he or she is face to face with such a being. The *qutub*, or spiritual pole as the Sufis have called it, is the perfect vehicle for God's love in the world. The teacher is the perfection of God's manifestation of love in time and space. Universal Man is more than the bringer of spiritual redemption cosmically and personally; such a being is the prototype of God on earth. God is indeed manifest in the guru as the guru is manifest in all. Jesus Christ proclaimed,

> *No man knoweth the Father except the Son,*
> *and whomsoever the Son revealeth Him unto.*

We in the West are often averse to seeing the need for a living spiritual Master. Yet in every other field of endeavor, we are hesitant to proceed without a teacher. We would shun a doctor or lawyer who had not taken the appropriate studies at an accredited institution with experts in the field. The refusal, in our culture, to accept a spiritual authority reflects our society's disregard for tradition. Sawan Singh, the great sage of Beas, once remarked that:

There is no contention about the clouds dispensing the rain.
No one expects the rain to come out of the clear blue sky.
Why then should not the perfect guide or mentor distribute
the rain of His mercy and grace?[11]

Sri Ramana Maharshi stated the same theme in his own idiom: "God and guru are not really different; they are identical."[12] By knowing the one, the disciple knows the other. Jesus said: "If ye had known me, ye should have known my Father also: and from henceforth ye know him, and have seen him." The guru who truly fulfills the role of "dispeller of darkness" is an inseparable ingredient on the spiritual path. It is the guru whose company provides "the keys which unlock the doors of Paradise" as Attar so rightly noted.

Drawn by the Master

An ironic twist of fate is that it is not the disciple who finds the teacher, but the Master who first loves the disciple and draws him or her to his feet. Bayazid al Bastami, a great Sufi Master of Persia, spoke of this strange paradox:

For a long time I was under the delusion that I loved Him.
But the truth is that it was He who first loved me.[13]

This somewhat strange reversal of roles is one of the great mysteries of the spiritual path. At the heart of this paradox is the notion that love is a gift of the Beloved and brings the disciple from selfhood to selflessness and from separation unto union. Kabir, the great sixteenth-century poet and Master, describes the condition of one who has realized this in his or her heart:

Kabir says to go and get the company of some saint.
Keep the company of Him who has controlled His mind.
Without measure will He give the wealth of Naam or love.
Shun the company of the worldly
Who may give you milk and honey.
I ask not for powers miraculous,
Kabir says, "Give me the Master's Darshan [company]
daily." [14]

Kabir's instructions may appear almost naive at first glance. Yet out of thousands of disciples who start the journey, only a rare few come to see the full significance of the God-man. Some spiritual traditions even state that the existence of the entire universe is predicated upon the presence of some perfect being in its midst. In the Jewish faith we find a similar notion in the concept of the thirty-six Zadikim, or perfect ones, without whose support the world would collapse.

So the *rasul* (intercessor) is the cohesive glue that cements the world together. It is light, love, and life for which the world was created, and without their manifest presence, existence has no purpose. The God-man represents the prototypical perfection that lies latent in each of us. Without the Masters' light shining in the vastness of this material darkness, the world itself would cease to exist. A God-intoxicated devotee tells us:

O Thou, the light of whose beauty has
Illuminated the beauties of this world.
The reflection of thy excellence has fallen on them.
Everywhere are found the manifestations of thy beauty.
In everyone is found the passion of thy love.[15]

After hearing about these great saints, it is natural that the would-be lover develops an interest in meeting and spending time in the company of one of them. Jesus said: "My sheep hear my voice, and I know them, and they follow me" (John 10:27). Coming to the feet of a Master is not an occurrence that is accidental or miraculous. It is the result of the Master's own love for the human concerned. It may appear that the disciple approaches the Master, but in reality it is the Master who draws the disciple to him.

Ascended Masters

Although most spiritual traditions acknowledge the role of a living spiritual guide, the cry of the soul never goes unheeded. The supreme power of love works in a myriad of ways, carefully tending to the evolution of each and every spark of divine light. While it is possible to contact past Masters for spiritual guidance, many esoteric texts confirm that it is unwise to rely solely on such sources, since direct revelation usually occurs only for a small minority of evolved souls.

In addition, ascended Masters usually choose to work through, and in cooperation with, the spiritual luminaries of the day. In this way, an unbroken transmission of light and power can be maintained across many generations. Finally, ascended Masters and adepts generally focus their guidance on those souls on the inner planes who require further assistance. Like a commander in the field, the living spiritual mentor is in a unique position to perceive and address the innumerable difficulties and needs that arise in the course of a disciple's journey.

Trial and Sacrifice

For most of us, the thirst for spiritual revelation involves much searching and, often, great suffering and anguish. Every scripture portrays this "valley of the shadow of death." This is the experience of the "dark night of the soul" in which the soul undergoes drastic and traumatic purification as it is prepared for its unveiling before the divine bride.

This suffering is a prerequisite for the encounter with the Beloved. But suffering is not undergone for its own sake; it exists only in order to prepare the soul for its heavenly journey. Just as the word "sacrifice" essentially means "to make sacred," so too suffering is a sort of interior fire, a *tapas*, as the Hindus call it, which removes that which is contingent from that which is essence. The sincere faith of the lover is always tested, because without trial or sacrifice the eyes of the bird of the soul remain fixed upon the carrion of the material world instead of the pearl of the Beloved's eye.

The consummation of this stage is accomplished when the lover arrives at the doorstep of the Beloved and is lucky enough to realize, in the words of Saint Alphonsus Liguori, a seventeenth-century Benedictine mystic,

> *How often has it happened that what we consider*
> *a punishment and chastisement of God,*
> *was a special work of grace, an act of His infinite mercy!*[16]

Following page:
The Pure Land
Musée Guimet, Paris

This eighteenth-century Japanese illustration depicts the palace of Skhavati. The palace, the Western Paradise of the Mahayana Buddhist sect, is rich with gold and gems. These are symbolic of the manifested light and beauty of this realm. Entry into this paradise is achieved only after passing through the fire of separation and subduing the hydra-headed serpent of desire. Yet for the true lover, the delights of heaven become insipid in comparison to the majesty and glory of the Divine Beloved.

Intimacy:
The Development of Remembrance

Hearer and heard as one in the Eternal Word.
— Meister Eckhart

*And I will bring forth in shining light those who have
loved my Holy Name and I will seat each on a throne of honor*
— The Book of Noah

Initiation

In the preceding stage, we saw how the spiritual guide becomes the embodiment of the lover's ideal and is in fact responsible for the first flickering of love that begins to smolder in the lover's heart. It is usually at this critical juncture that the disciple enters into a formal bond of spiritual fellowship known as *initiation* in most sacred traditions.

The subject of initiation is complex and involved, and in this chapter we will consider only its most important features as they relate to the development of the lover-Beloved relationship.

On its most literal level, initiation represents a formal acceptance by a teacher of a student into a specific spiritual order. Although each spiritual order will differ in outer rituals, the essence of initiation is the direct transmission of the spiritual power of the Master into the heart of the disciple. Spiritual power goes far beyond common practices like being given a certain mantra, the bestowal of a new name, or the acceptance into a church congregation.

Spiritual power involves a firsthand experience of inner divinity in the form of celestial light and inner rapturous music. Such experiences form the basis of any true initiation and have been referred to in all religious traditions. Christians have called it *baptism by fire;* Sufis, the *kalma-i-kalim;* Buddhists, *the sonorous sound;* Jews, *the Word;* and Hindus, *udgit.*

The details of this experience vary from person to person, but they represent an unbreakable bond of spiritual love, grace, and guidance between the Master and the disciple.

The full nature of this relationship is impossible to understand from the outside. The commitment on the part of the Master is a profound one, for the Master assumes the full weight of responsibility for the ultimate evolution of that soul. The nature of this responsibility is itself a grand mystery, and reveals itself only as the disciple matures in love and receptivity.

Initiation may be performed in a variety of ways. A formal initiation ceremony is no indication of whether one has received such a transmission. In *The Everything and the Nothing,* Meher Baba asserts that a truly competent saint can convey such a transmission through a glance or a gesture, or even from thousands of miles away. The perfect saint, in fact, is not constrained by time or space and can unleash the floodgates of grace to whomsoever he or she chooses, at any time.

In the past, according to Kabir, initiation was generally given only after a disciple has spent months or even years in the company of such a perfect being. In the closing years of the twentieth century, few, if any, have time to spend years in the company of a saint. In past ages, much inner work was required before a soul was deemed worthy of initiation. Today the gift of initiation is frequently given and the disciple is then asked to continue the work of inner purification subsequently.

During this stage of the journey, the would-be lover knows little of the true greatness of the Beloved and, though desirous of embarking upon this great quest, has little knowledge of the agony and torture that lie ahead of him or her. If our wayfarer is fortunate, he or she meets a true guide and receives the priceless gift of knowing his or her ever-present inner divinity.

The formal acceptance of a disciple into the spiritual brotherhood, through the process of initiation, is a prerequisite for the passage into the second phase of this stage, which we have called *intimacy*. This phase is called "the blind string of love" in *The Cloud of Unknowing*, a classic work on Christian contemplation by an unknown medieval author who well knew the potent forces that begin to stir in the heart of the disciple.

The Sufis of the school of Moinuddin Chisti have called it *sadaqa*—literally, "truth." I have thought it better to apply the word "sincerity" to its translation because this is, in fact, a phase in which one's loyalty and sincerity are severely tested.

Living in Close Proximity

The preliminary experience of this phase of intimacy is, as we noted earlier, a direct result of the Beloved's own love, which has been injected within the heart of the disciple. Later, as the seed of this love begins to grow, an overwhelming desire to live in close proximity to the Beloved seizes the lover's mind. In due course this results in the meeting of the lover with the spiritual Beloved, and time is spent in the court of the Beloved's graciousness.

During this period the lover generally loses his or her wits around the Beloved and is in simultaneous awe and fear of the Beloved. Every detail, every word, even the way the Beloved dresses and ties his or her shoes evokes awe and wonderment in the lover's heart. In the Jewish tradition it is said that a certain disciple was asked why he had come to study at the feet of the great Bal Shem Tov (Master of the Name). He replied, "To learn how he ties his shoes."

The lover's fascination with every aspect of the Beloved's life develops an intimate inner dialogue between soul and soul and heart to heart. The time spent during these days is the most treasured of all moments in the lover's life. During this phase, the Beloved showers seemingly limitless torrents of ecstasy upon the lover. The lover, in turn, nearly drowns in the sea of personal affection bestowed upon him or her.

These rare displays of personal intimacy, however, soon lay a trap for the lover, who now becomes enmeshed in what the

Sufis have called "the shackles of the Beloved's love." The poor lover, while enjoying the seemingly unending fiesta of the Beloved's lyrical glances, now begins to question his or her worthiness to receive them. From this moment on, the lover is slowly yet decisively made aware of his or her own shortcomings while the majesty of the Beloved steadily grows and grows.

In this way the lover is fashioned and molded by the Beloved's direct display of love. Gradually this dependency of the lover on the Beloved is increased to such an extent that the lover can no longer tolerate living apart from the Beloved's company. Since it is usually not in the hand of fortune for the lover always to be in the physical presence of the Beloved, the lover becomes distraught and anxious.

In due course, the lover's heart ripens and tears flow in sorrowful pleas to be reunited with the Beloved. If this phase matures, the Beloved may test the sincerity of the lover's cries by creating great hardships and obstacles to the fulfillment of the lover's desire. It is not unusual at this stage for the lover to undergo great tribulation in order to catch a mere passing glance from the cherished Beloved. Amir Khusrau, the poet and mystic of India, seems best to have summed up the state of humbleness and entreaty that envelops a lover:

I am on the verge of death,
Hasten to me that I may live.
Will it be of avail shouldst thou turn up when I die?[1]

In a similar passage in the *Adi Granth,* the sacred scriptures of the Sikhs, the poet remarks:

Without my Beloved I have no comfort
and I am weeping all alone. O Nanak, a wife
who does not meet her husband is miserable.

The story of Leila and Majnun wonderfully illustrates the condition of the lover enmeshed in the "shackles of love." Majnun greatly adored Leila, his beloved. One day a man who lived near Majnun saw him sifting the earth by the road and said, "Majnun, what are you looking for?"

"I am looking for Leila," he replied.

The man asked, "Do you hope to find Leila there?"

"I look for her everywhere," said Majnun, "in the hope of finding her somewhere." So, too, is the attitude of the true lover caught up in the spirit of the quest. After receiving the first draft of wine from the flagon of the Beloved's eyes, nothing matters except the pursuit of the lover's true aim. Attar described this state in these words:

> *Then he (the lover) will no longer fear the dragons, the*
> *guardians of the tenth door, which seek to devour him.*
> *When the door is opened and he enters,*
> *then dogma, belief and unbelief all cease to exist.*[2]

It is at this juncture that the dialectical nature of the lover's relationship, which is to characterize much of the subsequent journey, is first established. On the one hand, it is the lover who is seeking the Beloved, but in reality his or her love is merely a reflection of the "life-inspiring glances" of the Beloved. Though both share the same ontological reality as "essences of love," the lover is doomed to a role of abandonment, rejection, hopelessness, and poverty of spirit, while the Beloved is constantly increasing in grandeur, omnipotence, glorification, and indifference.

Although they appear to contradict each other they are, in fact, perfect mirrors of each other. The Beloved can only increase in beauty as the lover humbles himself or herself further. The seeming glory of the Beloved is no doubt perfect in itself, but cannot be realized in time and space without the appearance of the lover. The full mystery of this exchange is, however, a great secret and we shall deal with it more specifically later.

Telling the World

During the beginning phase of this stage, the lover, after experiencing something of the state of yearning, often expresses a newfound affection by *speaking about the Beloved* to every passerby. There is a well-known saying in mysticism that "He who loves a thing, speaks of it often." It is but natural in this state for the lover to express verbally what is uppermost in his or her mind. In due course the thread of remembrance is stitched between the lover and the Beloved, and the tapestry of their love is knitted in reciprocal knots of yearning and remembrance.

These are experienced in spurts at first and naturally so, for the lover has yet to be tested in his or her love. During these initial moments of heightened receptivity, the lover will receive direct inner transmissions from the Beloved.

Though these moments of ecstasy and inner attunement are brief, they will prove to be a seductive bait to lure the lover ever deeper into the heart of the Beloved. As this process continues, the lover begins to open his or her heart ever wider to the elevating and blissful dialogue with the Beloved.

Although it is well known that Jesus' disciples spread Christianity throughout the known world within just a few centuries of His ascension, it is not widely realized that the Master had them go on a much earlier round of preaching. Right after He had called them, at the very beginning of their three-year lover-Beloved relationship, He had them go out to "preach the good news" to all the towns in the area. Jesus was apparently well acquainted with the lover's need, very early in the process, to tell the world about the love that has dawned in his or her heart.

The Bonds of Fellowship

This phase reaches its maturation when two distinct movements occur. First, and of immediate importance, is the newly found *bond of fellowship* that the lover recognizes with his or her co-wayfarers. This is a direct result of the Beloved's living example of reciprocity and compassion, which pours forth effortlessly and in seemingly limitless measure.

The lover no longer relates to others as one entrenched in the confines of religious dogma, but opens his or her heart in spiritual brotherhood to all souls, whatever their faith or stage of inner development. Here there is no room for pretentious devotion that elevates one religion above another or which sacrifices the integrity of any living being. In the Sikh scriptures this truth is most poignantly captured:

This possessiveness has gone,
Since I got the radiation of the Master's company.
There is no enemy, no stranger,

All are now very dear to me.[3]

Wonder and Awe

The second phase of this station is characterized by a sense of wonder and awe, which dazzles and inebriates the lover. Having tasted the divine nectar of love pouring forth from the Beloved, the lover cannot fail to be wonder-struck. Bhai Nandlal Goya, a disciple of Guru Gobind Singh, has tried to give us some indication of this condition. He says:

Just to see Thy face again I once more took this physical form; otherwise what is there in this world for me; I have no interest in it. Those years are the best of my life which are spent in remembrance of Thee. Otherwise what was the use of my coming beneath this blue sky? What is there in the world for me? O Satguru, when I forget Thee, those moments are like death.[4]

In due course the disciple, by repeating the Master's name, or by lovingly remembering him, will "get intoxication, ecstasy and joy. Our hearts will dance at the very thought of Him."[5] As the remembrance of the lover increases, he or she witnesses all beauty and majesty personified in the being of the Beloved. One poet artfully explained this predicament:

Thou art the king of the realm of beauty,
I am a helpless beggar.

My life which is not my own has no asset
Except its sense of wonder.[6]

This quality of *wonder* arises directly from the divine bounty and fills the lover not only with the awe of the Beloved, but with a sense of his or her own nothingness as well. The paradox of this state, which is a continuous process, is the emptying of the cup of "I"-ness while being immersed in the cosmic presence.

Maria Vela, a little-known seventeenth-century Spanish mystic, overwhelmed once by her own nothingness, and deep in ecstatic prayer, seemed to hear Christ speak these comforting words: "This nothingness which you see yourself to be is what I love in you. From this nothingness you will ascend to the heights."[7]

Saint John the Baptist seems to have had a similar insight when face to face with his Divine Beloved. He said: "He must increase, but I must decrease" (John 3:30). This sense of wonder and awe is described in this koan by Li Liweng:

> First we look at the hills in the painting,
> Then we look at the painting in the hills.[8]

In the Tao Te Ching (XLVIII), we have a remarkably similar passage that cannot help to bring to mind how closely related these experiences must be:

> He who pursues learning will increase every day;
> He who pursues the Tao will decrease every day.
> He will decrease and continue to decrease,
> Till he or she comes at non-action;
> By non-action everything can be done.

Divine majesty is a recognizable feature of the landscape of this journey at this stage, and anyone who tastes of that abundance must find himself or herself emptied of the smallness of his or her separate self. The Greek word *metanoia*, translated in the Christian Bible as "repentance," literally means "turning away," but strongly implies "turning inward" as well. To be filled with divine presence implies the emptiness of our own form; one must replace the other if the duality of illusion is to be transcended. This involves a repentance of fear and a turning inward toward God's glory and Beauty.[9] In this context repentance (*teschubah* in Judaism) is the true healer and our true redeemer, and it "reaches to the throne of Glory" (Talmud).

The thread of remembrance gives the lover a look at the very tapestry of divine revelation. The name and the named are interwoven, like woof and warp. With every thread of remembrance the lover weaves, the magnificent tapestry of union grows. The encounter with the Beloved is the raison d'être for the lover.

Sant Darshan Singh speaks of this wondrous encounter with the zest of one who knows its depths:

I could neither find smiles in the flowers,
nor light in the stars,
Until I met you, O Beloved,
joy was nowhere to be found.[10]

What magic it is to behold the face of the Beloved, and what lover would not be enthralled by the springtime-producing smile of the Beloved? Indeed, the bewitching beauty of the Beloved is all too much for the lover to bear and even a momentary glimpse of the face of the Beloved leaves the lover wonder-struck, gasping for breath and life. In this perplexing condition, the madcap lover remains a mere string of memories, which the Beloved plucks and with which He plays havoc.

In the court of love of the lover's heart, it is beauty that presides, and the entire universe is revealed to be a playground for the sport of his or her lovemaking. Edward Young in his poem *Night Thoughts* captured this idea:

To reach creation; read its mighty plan
In the bare bosom of the Deity.
The plan and execution, to collide
To see before each glance of piercing thought
All cloud, all shadow, blown remote and leave.
No Mystery: but that of love divine.

Remembrance

The development of this *intense inner remembrance* of the Beloved is one of the profound turning points in the spiritual journey. Gratitude, faith, awe, and humility all flow unimpeded from the font of recollection and invocation. There is a pre-temporal connection between the name and the named. The former is the essence and the latter its attributes in time and space.

In the realm of time the name of the Beloved is the connecting link to the Beloved. The repetition of any name of God produces in its wake a certain measure of union. By repeating the names of the Beloved, the lover invokes not only the spirit of prayer and supplication but the very essence of that inner presence as well. The outer word purifies and cleanses the receptacle of the lover's heart until the inner essence of love, which is "the true light," manifests itself.

There may be a thousand names of God, and each religion has its own unique manner in which the Divine Beloved is addressed. But in all cases it is the supreme nameless and formless Being who receives those calls and responds accordingly, no matter which religion or faith the lover professes. The very act of invoking the name of the Beloved establishes sympathetic bonds of communication between the one and the many.

In Eastern Orthodox Christianity, which has gained greater popularity in recent years, the initiate might recite the Jesus prayer, which is the simple yet heartfelt repetition of the words, "Jesus Christ, Son of God, have mercy on me, a sinner." Or, in simplified version, just the name of Jesus, or "It is the Lord" (John 21:7). In Sufism, this remembrance is termed *zikhr* and involves a repetition of the Islamic prayer *"La ilaaha'illa 'Llah Hu"* (literally, "There is no divinity except God"). The recitation of "the supreme name" *(a'zham)* is enjoined "with humility and in secret," and also "through fear and through desire" (Qur'an VII, 55–56). And again, "Is it not through remembrance of God that hearts are at rest and security?" (Qur'an XIII, 28).

In the Jewish scriptures, "The desire of our soul is to Thy name and the remembrance of Thee" (Isaiah 25:8). The renowned German mystic Jacob Boehme extolled the untold power of invoking God's name when he said, "In the sweet name of Jesus Christ the whole process is contained." Indeed, this process of inner remembrance of the Beloved becomes the very life-breath of the lover.

Tulsi Das, renowned sixteenth century Bhakti poet and author of the Hindi *Ramayana*, considered the repetition of Ram's name the *sine qua non* of all spiritual practice. He praises not only the glory of the outer name but simultaneously the splendor of the true name of God within. Tulsi Das writes:

Of the servants who repeats the Name of Ram with love.
How can the unsurpassable wonders then be told.[11]

In a similar passage in the Bhagavad Gita, the most holy scripture of the Hindus, Lord Krishna declares to Arjuna: "If you devote your mind to me, I promise you will become absorbed in me." The Hindu, like the Christian or Sufi, in invoking the name of God, abandons his or her own existence for that of his or her Lord. The lover who has invoked the holy of holies experiences the divine form itself, as his or her heart opens and closes like the lotus before the sun of existence. By this invocation, the lover invites the divine presence to enlighten every fiber of his or her being.

The Buddhist, when he or she invokes the divine name of the Buddha Amitabbha, "enters into the golden halo of mercy" and finds security in the blessed light that Buddha called "the sonorous sound." As Frithjof Schuon has made clear, "Amida is Light and Life; His name carries the faithful towards the Western Paradise (Sukhavagt); the faithful allows the solar name through to its consummation, to the west—he follows it right 'into the beyond' leaving the world behind him in the night—he follows this sun which having traversed the 'round of existence' is thus gone (*tathagata*), or which is 'gone, gone not to return, gone to the other shore's gate' (*paragate, parasamgate*)."[12]

This short survey lists some of the ways in which different cultures use the name of God in prayer and meditation to remind them of their spiritual discipline.

Meditation on Meeting a Guide

In many religious traditions, the first step the seeker must take, after undergoing the necessary preliminary preparation, is to choose a guide or spiritual friend. As we have indicated, it may take a lifetime of preparation to enter into a relationship with such a being.

Accepting a spiritual friend into one's life is a profound decision, and the meditation below is, in part, a way of testing the ground before embarking upon such a relationship. The choice of guide is a momentous decision, not to be entered into lightly. The wrong choice could result in permanent scars to the soul.

This exercise will help to clarify and bring into focus the "archetypal Beloved" that is right for you. In Jungian terms, this would imply bringing forth from the collective unconscious the image of perfection and beauty that most resonates with your own inner propensities, background, and capacities as a human being.

In a mythological context, we are envisioning the supreme hero, saint, or Divine Beloved, the being who, as Joseph Campbell has suggested, has the power to transform and transfigure everyday pathos into mythos. This exercise is designed to be a means of attunement to the great sea of potentiality within which we all live and breathe.

There is a powerful story about the response of a destitute prostitute as she encounters her Beloved for the first time. Here is how she describes Him:

> *His mouth was like the heart of a pomegranate, and the shadows in his eyes were deep. And He was gentle, like a man mindful of his own strength. In my dreams I beheld the kings of the earth standing in awe in His presence. I would speak of His face but how shall I? It was like night without darkness and like day without the noise of day. It was a sad face and it was a joyous face. And well I remember how once He raised His hand toward the sky and His parted fingers were like the branches of an elm. And I remember Him pacing the evening. He was not walking. He Himself was road above road;,even as a cloud above the earth that would descend to refresh the earth. But when I stood before Him and spoke to Him ,He was a man and His face was powerful to behold. And He said to me, "What would you, Miriam?" I did not answer Him but my wings enfolded my secret, and I was made warm. Because I could bear His light no more, I turned and walked away, but not in shame. I was only shy, and I would be alone, with His fingers upon the strings of my heart.*

Allow this image to stay awhile in your heart and thoughts. Then, as the image fades, picture the Master in this story facing you. Capture the emotional intensity of the meeting and make it your own.

For the meditation below, choose a quiet spot, either alone, or in the company of spiritual friends, after you have put to rest the "everydayness" of the world. You should restrain your senses and remain aloof from emotional upheavals for a period of time. If possible, create a prolonged period of "sacred space" in which you can turn within to meet your Beloved. For the American Indians, all nature was sacred; their temple was the sky overhead and the earth below. In whatever form best works for you, create a simple, quiet, holy ground for these exercises.

After making yourself quite comfortable, bring your mind to focus on the image of the Beloved. It does not matter whether you have ever met your Beloved before; all you need is to long for the personification of this One in whatever form he or she may take.

Allow your whole body to relax completely. Feel the preoccupations of the day floating gently away from you as you are enfolded in your own sacred space.

Allow your mind to fade to gray, and provide the mental space for your own divine friend to appear. Begin the process by visualizing the activities of the friend as he or she might go through daily life. As the friend walks, imagine his or her gestures. Does the friend float across the earth; does he or she glide, or just stroll?

Bring to focus now, as you imagine this being, how the friend interacts with people. Does he or she bow, raise the hands in prayer, or simply shake your hand? Does this being smile as you approach?

Now imagine this being opening up to you. What does the friend say to you as you meet? What exact words does he or she use? Listen closely. How, exactly, does your friend speak? Are his or her words gentle or firm? Are they soft, musical, compassionate, or simply sweet and humble?

Imagine your first glance at the friend's face. What questions arise in your mind? What doubts? What thoughts cross your mind as he or she talks and looks at you? Do you speak? What goes on inside you? Examine yourself closely.

Examine your friend closely; focus intently upon him or her. What arises in your heart of hearts as you open up to your friend? Are you longing for him or her? Are you apathetic, joyous, or nervous? Examine your feelings, your responses. Examine your doubts. Be totally honest about your feelings.

While you hold those thoughts in your mind, gently awake from the meditation. Know that the dream was more real than any act or meeting you have ever known.

Know that you have met your Beloved, if only for a moment, and that meeting, which was outside of time, must one day enter time. The Beloved is the very life of our life and the more we awake, the more we move in our friend's being.

Following page:
Rama Shoots Arrow at Radha
Metropolitan Museum of Art, New York

In this detail from a lively Hindu drawing, Rama aims his bow at Radha, attempting to wound her with the joys of love, while Krishna is summoned (not shown). The arrow that pierces the lover is unique in that it never goes deep enough to slay the her or his individuality. Instead, it remains embedded in the lover's heart, never allowing the lover to forget the Beloved. Both Radha and Krishna are in essence one, and eventually this intrinsic identification is realized by the lover. Sur Das speaks on behalf of Radha: "You become Radha and I will become Madhava, truly Madhava (Krishna). This is the reversal which I shall produce."

4

CHAPTER

Sincerity:
The Vale of Tears

Let us toss in pain,
Why think now of sleep?
We have a night that has no dawn.

—Sant Darshan Singh

The return to the primordial state of at-one-ment and gnosis is a return through a valley of the most intense pain. This
process could well be called, in Keats' phrase, the "vale of
tears." These tears represent, both literally and symbolically, the
purifying process at work. At the very simplest level of meaning, tears represent the recognition by the soul of its separate
and fragmented existence.

The lover is deep into the primordial quest for the essential
rebirth or rediscovery of the animating and revivifying process
of what Carl Jung called "self-individuation." Something must
die in this process in order for the new spirit to unfold, purified
and pristine. That something is the attachment to sensory pleasures, impure desires, and meaningless and prideful pursuits.

This stage is the *apatheia*, or purification, of the early
Christian fathers and the practice of *pratyahara* (restraint of the
senses) of the Yogasutras. During this stage the lover is required

to withdraw his or her sense organs and develop contentment and internal concentration.

Tears are a wonderful symbol of this aspect of the journey, for such tears arise from the molten depths of the lover's yearning and pathos. As the lover polishes the mirror of his or her heart, powerful currents of love begin to surge in his or her veins burning to ashes everything except the object of one's love. This internal burning in time becomes the very inner essence of the lover's condition.

During this station, four fascinating developments occur, which mark successive degrees of purification. First is the recognition of the Beloved's beauty. Second comes profuse tears. The third is characterized by intense regret and agitation. And lastly, the thought of the Beloved seizes the mind of the lover.

In many respects, this stage is simply the first act of a long and bittersweet play of separation that is to follow. But few lovers at this point have even the slightest hint of the agony awaiting them. The beauty of the Beloved has so captured their hearts and so bewitched their senses that the path ahead of them remains veiled and concealed. For a lover, intoxicated by endless streams of love, light, and beauty, which appear to emanate effortlessly from the Beloved, no such long view is possible. The eyes of the lover see the Beloved as the very fountainhead of beauty in the world. This recognition is the first of these phases. A gnostic tells us his own story:

> *Everything is illuminated by the Beauty of Thy face,*
> *Every man of heart is desirous of Thee only,*
> *O bestower of unique Beauty,*
> *Who bestows on the deserving,*
> *All are really lovers of Thy beauty only.*[1]

The inner vision of the Divine Beloved is not, however, vouchsafed to the lover until his or her appreciation for the grandeur of the Beloved reaches an apex of longing. Such yearning cannot be attained until the lover forgoes all other pleasures for the vision of the Beloved. Life has no meaning unless it be embedded in the context of the Beloved's love. The cry of the helpless lover at this stage is:

Would that I would forget all pleasures
Save the pleasure of Thy love.
And the pain of Thy life replace the life in me.[2]

The Vale of Tears

The second phase of this station, which spontaneously follows the first, is called *the vale of tears*. During this phase, the lover nearly drowns in a sea of tears, which appear to gush up from an inexhaustible well within his or her being. In conjunction with this, there appears an agitation and restlessness is relieved only by the physical presence of the Beloved or by an act of pure revelation from within. All outer pleasure becomes insipid and meaningless. The lover cries for the transcendent rapture of the Divine Beloved, and nothing else will satisfy his or her longing.

During this phase, there may be "yelling, howling, and lamentation, because love has not yet taken over the whole of the lover's being." But as Ahmad Ghazzali (Al-Ghazzali's brother) notes, "Once the affair reaches perfection, and love conquers the lover's domain of being, then these things are withheld, and lamentation is replaced by observation [of the Beloved's form], and leanness [of the lover's existence], because impurity has been replaced by purity." Ghazzali describes the process in these words:

> *In the beginning when I was a novice in love,*
> *My neighbor could not sleep at night from my whimpers.*
> *But now that my pain has increased,*
> *my whimpering has decreased.*
> *When fire takes over something completely,*
> *smoke dwindles.*[3]

The Christian saint, John of Ruysbroeck, in his masterpiece *Spiritual Espousals*, describes in great detail the unique and baffling state in which the lover finds himself or herself after some period in this station.

> *The lover, after receiving the call to unity with the inner*
> *Christ, and after tasting this transport of love, experiences*
> *an interior restlessness which will scarcely practice or heed*

the dictates of reason, unless it obtains what it loves. This interior transport consumes a person's heart and drinks his blood. The heat which is here felt from within is the most intense of a person's entire life. His corporeal nature is secretly wounded and consumed without being acted upon from outside, and the fruit of the virtues ripens more quickly than in all the modes which have previously been described.[4]

In this state of inner restlessness and oblivion, the lover may experience intense sorrow or the sweetest joy. However, neither experience lasts long and both often appear inwardly as one. One unknown poet wrote that it was "as if the entire body were being consumed from within by an interior fire and the yearning of the heart pours out the eyes like the sap from burning wood." These torrents of tears are often uncontrollable, and yet the true lover has not an ounce of self-pity but is rather propelled by the tears to make greater and greater sacrifices for the Beloved.

In the ancient Vedic scriptures, one of the Gujarti hymns cautions those who think they might avoid the inevitable "crucible of fire":

The pathway of love is the ordeal of fire.
The shrinkers turn away from it.
Those who take the plunge into the fire attain eternal bliss.
Those who stand far off looking on
are scorched by the flame.
Love is a priceless thing only to be won at the cost of death.
Those who live to die, these attain,
For they have shed all thoughts of self. [5]

In the mystic literature of the East, pearls are often used as a symbol for tears. These tears are pearls of great importance, for they contain all the secrets of love itself. The anguish of separation produces tears, which initiate a welling up of the soul into a state of supreme concentration. This crystallization of concentration within the soul is an act of perfect prayer, for it reconnects the soul with the Divine Beloved. In this sense, the psychology of purification is the act of perfecting prayer or dialogue with God. The profusion of tears that any true lover sheds paves the way for ultimate union with the Beloved:

I did not weep until my heart was lost.
So strange the bartering of love appeared.
I gave the shining jewel of my soul,
To buy these pearls my tears.

Rabia Basri, a celebrated Muslim woman saint, was once asked whether her prayers started first and then God came, or if God came and she then started to cry. She replied, "The moment tears burst out of my eyes I realize that the rain-laden clouds have come; I start my prayers and I find God there."

Tears, then, are a gift of grace from the Divine Beloved because they are the flowers that precede the fruit of union. As with the Buddhist state of "mindfulness," in which the desires of the soul are temporarily abated, the oscillations of the mind come to a halt. Of course, the mind may yet be active on much more subtle levels, unperceived by the conscious mind. However, in both instances, the mind has been brought to a state of relative stillness and experiences a wholly new perception of reality. The conscious mind achieves a new unity and singleness. At the same time the unconscious mind has come closer to the eye of inspection and the knife of a discerning intellect.

Inner Restlessness

The fruit of this phase ripening in the heart of the lover is an *inner restlessness*. Once the lover has experienced this state of inner bliss, the soul is restless to return to it once again. Each new encounter with the Divine Beloved produces a greater sense of agitation. Sant Kirpal Singh remarked that when this remembrance of the divine becomes overpowering, "there is no sleep for the eyes, no rest for the joints, for such a person can have no peace unless he sees his Beloved."[6]

Another poet observed: "Oh, mathematicians, you have calculated how long is the day, the night, the year; how long is the night for the anguished heart which cries for its Beloved?" The seeker experiencing this state cries out:

Without seeing the Beloved, sleep does not come;
This separation has now become unbearable.[7]

Often, while passing through this state, a seeker is advised by well-intentioned friends to cease the searching and desiring for God that is causing such discomfort. But the seeker has no choice, for his or her heart has been scorched for all time. Guru Amar Das, the fourth guru of the Sikhs, when passing through his state, rebuked his friends,

Do not utter such words,
for even in this pain, there is sweetness.

This burning restlessness is part of the process through which every true seeker passes to some degree. Kabir was aware of the necessity for weeping and discontent:

Whosoever got Him, did so with tears;
could He be had with laughter and joy,
none would be without Him.[8]

Ancient writers made a distinction between two types of tears: "Tears which develop through love for the Beloved, which are shed for your Beloved are called *ann-soo;* they are real tears. Tears caused by disappointment, unhappiness, or disillusion with worldly mundane affairs are called *een-soo;* the latter are not tears in the world of mysticism."[9]

If we study the lives of saints, we will find in many of them a period when they wept profusely while experiencing the pain of separation. It is said of the Prophet Mohammed that he would humbly say: "O Allah, bless us with a weeping eye." In the Indian tales of Krishna the *gopis* (God-intoxicated lovers) shed many a tear in divine longing for Krishna.

Tears, then, represent a perfect conclusion to, and about-face from, the previous period of *intimacy.* The lover, who at first coveted the priceless blessing of the Master's personal affection, now treasures his or her own burning tears. It is not that the personal attention of the Master is not appreciated when it is experienced. But the lover's primary nutriment now comes from the molten waves of love from his or her own being.

Regret

The results of this process develop into the *third phase of sincerity* which we call *regret*. The word "regret" usually implies a lost opportunity. But in the present context "regret" means a deepening of the feelings of separation and a fear of being deprived of the inner blessings of the Beloved. A poet in describing this state remarks:

O my divine Beloved!
Why hast Thou thrown me afar from Thee
and deprived me of the constant downpour of Thy blessings
and engaged me with the devil and in following
my Carnal self?[10]

This phase of intense regret has several specific aspects to it. The twelfth-century Sufi saint Al-Ghazzali gives us a vivid description of some of the more pronounced characteristics of this phase.

First, he says, the lover does not lament any loss in the world besides that of the remembrance of the Lord. And if, for a moment, he or she forgets the Lord, the lover prays to the Lord to be forgiven that transgression. Quoting Hazrat Abu Bakar, Al-Ghazzali notes that "he who has tasted of the Divine Love, is stopped from desiring anything in the world or seeking the company of any individual." A third aspect of this regret is the sleeplessness that gradually overtakes the lover. Ghazzali notes, "He who claims to love Me, and yet sleeps at night lost to himself and his surroundings, he is false in his profession of love for Me, and has not felt separation, for he seeks not Me, but his own self-indulgence, and that is not the way of lovers."[11]

Seized by the Thought of the Beloved

This phase of deep regret inevitably leads to a state of perfect remembrance, in which the mind is completely and continuously *seized by the thought of the Beloved*. When the inner mind has become sufficiently purified through the constant repetition of the Beloved's name, or some attribute of the Beloved, the appearance of the inner radiant or light form of the Master makes its appearance.

The link between these two states should be clearly understood by the lover, for it is a subtle key to the whole journey that has yet to unfold. By bringing the image of the Beloved to mind, the lover sets up a powerful thought-form connecting himself or herself to the Beloved.

These thought-forms, or "elementals," as the Christian gnostic and healer Daskalos has explained, possess a life of their own. They create from the ethereal energy of the universe a wholly new psychic and emotional reality for the lover. As this remembrance is literally etched upon the physical and subtle mind through constant repetition, it becomes part and parcel of the lover's noetic or causal body. Whatever becomes imprinted at the causal level must in fact be manifested as a physical and gross reality. However, this process is possible only when it is accompanied by an intense aspiration arising from the heart of the lover. Thought alone is insufficient. Only a heart that is agonized in longing can create such entirely new realities.

At this point, the thought of the Beloved literally seizes the lover, wherever and whatever he or she is doing. The lover has aligned his or her entire existence to coordinate with the Beloved's. The two beings, though perhaps separated by thousands of miles, remain in *constant telepathic communication* without the least bit of effort.

The lover who has arrived through the corridor of sincerity has been thoroughly tested on the grindstone of love. He or she has moved unfailingly through deep despair and endless weeping to agitation and mercurial restlessness, which appears to be without end. Intense regret has produced sleeplessness and constant repetition of the Beloved's name. Cleansed of ephemeral desires and self-indulgence, the lover, steadied, plunges headlong into the ocean of remembrance of the Beloved. Finally, the lover offers himself or herself into the crucible of fire and tastes the depth of real separation.

Following page:
Krishna Lifts Mount Govardhan
Metropolitan Museum of Art, New York

According to the legend depicted in this ca. 1590 Mughval illustration, the young god Krishna asserted His power over the god Indra (god of rain) by convincing the gopis (His lovers) near Mount Govardhan to worship the spirit of the mountain, into which He transformed Himself. Enraged by the upstart god, Indra raised up a terrible storm, threatening the land and the people. In response to the gopi's please, Krishna here lifts Mount Govardhan on His little finger and protects them from the storm. To the mystic lover this story reflects the unflinching faith that any true lover has in his or her Beloved. The story also points to the fact that even Indra is powerless before the supreme power of love.

CHAPTER

The Fire of Separation

I find my life beguiled into sorrow
And I am as one who is neither living nor dead.
I wander asking of You, O Beloved,
And they treat me as one who is crazed.

—Sant Kirpal Singh

In fourth stage of the journey, sometimes called *the fire of separation*, four movements occur that mark phases in the evolution of the process of separation.

First, the heart of the lover experiences an acute sense of *inner burning* that consumes all save the thought of the Beloved. In the second phase, the *constant invocation* of the Beloved's name produces an intense and perfect concentration in the living moment.

In the third phase, the trials and tortures of love are *transmuted into the cure for separation*. In this phase, everything, including the harshest of suffering, viewed as a special boon from the Beloved. In the last phase, the lover moves from willing resignation to a conscious *surrender* of all aspects of his or her life. In the last phase, since the door of union is not open and the lover cannot take nutriment directly from the Beloved, oppression becomes the lover's most valued sustenance. Here oppression does not imply physical torture, but rather the indifference and humiliation experienced at the hands of the Beloved.

Inner Burning

The symbol of love at this stage is *fire,* for the lover not only is burning, but he or she has become nothing but a flame of yearning. Some ancient authorities refer metaphorically to the face of the lover being inflamed with the image of the Beloved. For him or her, good and evil have ceased to exist. Farid-ud-din-Attar, author of *The Conference of the Birds,* describes this phase appropriately:

> *In this valley love is represented by fire & reason by smoke.*
> *When love comes, reason disappears.*
> *Reason cannot live with the folly of love.*
> *Love has nothing to do with human reason.*[1]

One who has been tested in the fire of love begins to realize the necessity of separation, for the very process of separation brings the lover into the embrace of the Beloved. For the lover, the moments in which he or she is acutely aware of individuality and hence separation are excruciating. In the Christian scriptures, this fire of longing is beautifully expressed in the Song of Songs, a book so unfashionably passionate and erotic that it offends many Christians. The Catholic church completely ignores it. But when interpreted as a document of the mystic's passion for God, the eroticism of this book is realized simply as the closest human analogy for unquenchable thirst for God. In this fire that consumes the lover's being, she cries out (Song of Songs 3:1–2):

> *Upon my bed by night*
> *I sought him whom my soul loves;*
> *I sought him, but found him not;*
> *I called him but he gave no answer,*
> *I will rise now and go about the city,*
> *In the streets and in the squares;*
> *I will seek him whom my soul loves.*

Such periods of *heartbreak*, as Rabbi Nachman expressed it, are the very essence, in Judaism, of turning our face to God. He described these periods of intense inner yearning as "screaming to God." The great Hasidic Master was also quick to point out that there is a world of difference between "heartbreak" and "depression."[2] In the former state, one is in a state of self-forgetfulness and spiritual yearning; in the latter one is consumed in the quicksand of self-delusion and despair. The difference here is critical for the disciple to understand, for the former implies the abandonment of associations with the world, while the latter enmeshes one further in the illusion of self-infatuation.

When the lover reaches this phase of intense inner aspiration, every second becomes agonizing, for there is no peace without a glimpse of the Beloved. In this state the lover calls out with heartrending cries, pleading for help and grace. In this state, even one moment without such remembrance of the Beloved is "like a death"[3] for the lover. Such intense longing produces a perfect cleansing of the mind's mirror.

With the passage of time, this phase culminates in a profound reorientation of the lover's faculties of perception and understanding. In the course of this mysterious inner alchemy, the lover realizes, in the words of Sant Kirpal Singh, that "what you see is *you*." In such a state, the lover who wants to see himself or herself will see only the image *(pakyar)* of the Beloved. A poet aptly describes this visionary experience:

I have your image in my eye so much,
that whatever I perceive, I think it is you.[4]

In such a condition, every atom appears endowed with the image of the Beloved. The greater the yearning, the greater will be the experience of this state. Such states of bittersweet separation are in fact orchestrated by the Beloved Himself. Hazur Baba Sawan Singh, a saint of the twentieth Century, maintains that "whom He [the Master] loves the most is always sent away for a while." Only in this way can the pangs of separation reach the pitch of yearning necessary to still the continuous oscillations *(vrittus)* of the mind.

For the true lover "time itself is an enemy, for it deludes one into thinking that life is endless." However, the lover knows the value of each moment and cherishes it as a sublime gift. Every moment is an opportunity to remember the Beloved. And every moment spent in forgetfulness of God is like a miniature death, for time cannot be reversed. In this sense every moment utilized for its highest purpose is immortalized, for it achieves the perfection of its potential.

A story about Kabir relates how he forgot the name of God twice. As a result of this loss, he wept inconsolably the whole night. Toward dawn, Lord Ram Himself came down to comfort Kabir and to assure him that He was well pleased with His disciple's unflagging love and practice. Kabir, still uncomforted, replied, "I have missed two opportunities to say the name of Ram. Never can I regain the joy of those lost names."[5] It is not difficult to find similar passages in other scriptures. The Sikh Bible, the *Gurmat Siddhant*, contains a remarkably similar account:

> To cease His remembrance, even for a second,
> All happiness leaves and misery results.
>
> My mind is desiring Thy Darshan:
> Like the rainbird in anguish,
>
> The thirst remains unquenched—there is no peace,
> I am living like that without the Beloved's Darshan
> [company].

Merging in the Moment

For the lover experiencing these pangs of separation, all apprehension about the future or the past drops off like autumn leaves in the wind. So intense is the concentration in the present that it produces a *merging in the moment*. One becomes, as the great Rumi once said, "The son of the moment."

It is this coming into the present that the ordeal of separation produces. And paradoxically, it is precisely here—in the present moment—that eternity is found. For the experience of separation appears infinite to the lover. He or she becomes lost in its timelessness. There is no escaping it. In this timelessness the lover finds not only the face of his or her Beloved, but the face of eternity as well. As the Zen master Seppo said,

If you want to know what eternity means, it is no further than this moment. If you fail to catch it in this present moment, you will not get it, however many times you are reborn in hundreds of thousands of years.[6]

The Cure for Separation

When separation itself seems endless, and the awareness of the lover becomes centered in the present moment, it becomes its own cure. At its zenith, the process of separation produces, to the lover's surprise, a state of intense inner bliss. This bliss is a further deepening of the process of self-abandonment. Since there is nothing left for the lover to take nutriment from, and union is still not possible, the lover finds himself or herself at the table of love and feasts upon his or her own pain. A poet by the name of Hawa describes this condition graphically:

None enjoy such luxury as I enjoy in Thy love,
My companion is pain, my wine is blood,
My rissole is the heart
My hors d'oeuvre is woe.

This state, though difficult to recognize because of its paradoxical nature, has been referred to in various religious scriptures. In the Christian scriptures, Saint Paul refers to being made perfect in his weakness. The cosmic and deeply personal significance of his suffering is made clear to him when he quotes the words of Jesus Christ (the only time he does so in all his voluminous writings): "my grace is sufficient for thee: for my strength is made perfect in weakness." (2 Corinthians 12:9)

In this state Paul cries out (2 Corinthians 12:10):

For the Sake of Christ then,
I am content with weakness, insults,
hardships, persecutions and calamities;
for it is when I am weak that I am strong.

Although Paul may not explicitly state that pain is desirable, he nevertheless implies that torment is an ingredient in gaining his perfection. If there is a difference here, it is simply in the mode of resignation and not in kind. The poet Hawa not only accepts his anguish but actually derives pleasures from it. He has surrendered to the process completely and exhibits no sign of personal preference. In Saint Paul's case, pain and anguish are only different aspects of an endless flow of blessings experienced as he surrenders to the Divine Beloved. The language may be different, but the theology and results are quite similar.

Constant Invocation

Such a condition gradually evolves into a continual prayer, which is unlike prayer as we normally describe it. This continual or *incessant prayer* involves no ordinary associations with the world and actually is embedded in the deepest humility. The Sufis have called this phase *hawa,* or intense supplication, but in reality it is more than simply "asking." It is also *affirming* the divine identity and the cosmic embrace of the Beloved.

The effectiveness of this supplication depends directly upon the sincerity and humility in which it is offered. If it contains even the slightest association with the world, it is flung back into the face of the lover. The lover has to be, as Saint Ignatius Loyola has said, "a true renouncer, renouncing all other thoughts except that which he loves."

In due course, the lover realizes that it is clearly not a matter in which he or she has any say. However, rather than turn away from the Beloved (as some unfortunately do), the lover surrenders the whole affair into the hands of the Beloved. This act of surrender produces a profound sense of endurance and resignation.

The lover soon realizes that any yearning that does not touch the deepest level of the heart is a prey to the tyranny of time. The path of love demands constancy and unlimited *patience* on the part of the lover. It is here that many a lover rolls in the seas of doubt and despair. The reason for the flight of the Beloved is that union with Him is not an insignificant matter. Using the female gender for the Beloved, Ahmad Ghazzali explains that "just as the lover must submit himself [to the Beloved] so that he is no longer himself, the Beloved must also consent to his being Her lover. So long as She has not consumed him entirely from inside and taken him as part of Herself, and so long as She has not received him completely, She escapes from him."[7] When, however, the lover has been completely tamed by love, then *he or she no longer wills even his or her own union with the Beloved.* Shah Latiff, a Hindu mystic of the fifteenth century, gives us some inkling of this endurance in the following lines:

> *True lovers love and adorn themselves*
> *with the scaffold as garments,*
> *And consider it a matter of shame*
> *to hesitate and lag behind,*
> *They accept by troth,*
> *wagering their life for it.*
>
> *A hundred times a day they rush to climb it [the gallows].*
> *Bidding good-bye to comforts,*
> *they suffer cheerfully to woo love.*[8]

Mira Bai, a female saint of the sixteenth century, expressed this theme with similar pathos:

> *Kahn (Her Master) I bought.*
> *The price he asked I gave.*
> *Some cry, "'Tis great" and others jeer, "'tis small."*
> *I gave in full, weighted to the utmost grain,*
> *My love, my life, my soul, my all.*[9]

The embrace of this endurance is so profound that every so-called obstacle appears to be another gift from the Beloved. The lover, as Meister Eckhart once said, includes all occurrences in his or her being, seeing them all as part of God's being.

For the lover experiencing this truth, whatever he or she pushes aside is exactly that part of himself or herself that most needs to be dealt with. Jung talks about how humans thrust away the dark side of their nature, refusing to acknowledge or explore it. This is precisely the area, however, that can teach us the most.

For the lover experiencing this truth, whatever is happening, both the seeming light and the seeming dark, is God's gift. Whatever the lover excludes is that aspect of God that he or she has not integrated within himself or herself. It is at this critical moment that *the will of the Beloved and the will of the lover begin to merge.*

Resignation

In the last phase of this passage through the fire of separation, called *resignation*, the lover consumes both union and separation. The lover realizes that both union and separation have in essence nothing to do with a love that is beyond constraints and phenomenal appearances. It is in this context that real surrender is understood and attained by the lover. Surrender is not some sort of passive defeat. Quite the contrary, *surrender represents the soul's dynamic and co-creative role in the will of God.* The mystic now has a new place in the scheme of creation.

Many Western readers equate the word "surrender" with giving in. But to the mystic, "surrender" means giving up the limited will in order to participate in the cosmic will. It is a highly conscious and supremely powerful act in which God embraces the lover as a conscious co-worker in the divine plan. The immensity of this act releases powerful currents of love into creation. The lover is at last, by providing God with a responsive channel for His creativity, augmenting the force of the creative impulse as it applies to this planet.

It is a curious fact that whether one is following the eightfold path of Buddha, the path of non-dualism of Sankara or Ramana Maharshi, or the path of love of Kabir and Nanak, all paths begin to resemble one another at this point.

For in essence, all paths lead to a state of intense resignation to the supreme will of the Creator. Once the lover resigns everything into the hands of the Beloved, the question of choice is no longer a possibility. Choice exists only when the illusion of separateness and therefore individuality prevails. As soon as the reality of a state of pure unity is known, the question of individual action separate from the divine is a blasphemy.

Seen from this vantage point the greatest "sin" is not action but ego. Ego, or "I-ness," presupposes the possibility of individual action. Transcending ego, there remains no other door for the lover to open, no other direction in which to look but into the face of the Beloved. Shah Latiff expresses this theme with great clarity when he says, "every fiber of the lover is turned into a veritable string of the guitar, which repeats His name every moment. He never complains or utters a sigh." Saint Paul refers to "I in Christ, and Christ in me."

To touch and heal those places in the heart of the lover which as yet have not been touched by love requires the magical touch of the teacher. For it is the Beloved alone who knows exactly where those areas are and how best to heal them. Lovers who understand this secret joyfully submit to the rebukes and trials that the Beloved may place in their path.

In the Christian tradition, so long as the individual characteristics of the lover remain, union with the Christ power is not possible. Crucifixtion, in this sense, is the obliteration of the outer characteristics of the lover and their replacement by those of the Beloved.

Following page:
Abraham Sacrificing Isaac
Conde Museum, Chantilly

In this detail from a Danish Psalter, Abraham is depicted being called to a test of faith. He is asked to sacrifice his only son, Isaac. During the stage of violent affection for the Beloved, the lover is called upon to sacrifice his or her reasoning, and to withhold judgement.

Fili devs prouidebit

pater ecce ignis z ligna ubi est uictima holocausti.

CHAPTER 6

Violent Affection

Love is the name for a continuous restlessness of the heart,
This endless yearning is the symbol of my life.
— Sant Darshan Singh

The fifth station of love has been termed *violent affection* by Sufis, *unceasing prayer* by Christians and *effortless insight* by Buddhists. This stage is also marked by four distinct aspects, according to the Sufi tradition. First is spontaneous and immediate *obeying of the commands* of the Beloved without thought or consideration. Second is the *expansion of the heart*, in which all creation is seen as a manifestation of the supreme being. Third comes *guarding the heart*, in which the lover carves every bit of reason or rationality from his or her being. Fourth is the *concealment of love* and the veiling of the secrets of love from all but the Beloved.

Spontaneous Obedience

In the first phase of this passage of violent love, the lover subjugates his or her reason and will entirely to the will of the Beloved. Having come to see through intense self-analysis the falsity of his or her own belief systems, he or she learns to withhold intellectual and personal judgment. The very thought of disobedience here is a departure from the court of

love. To understand this, one must realize that reason itself
cannot enter the abode of love. A saint named Baba Farid said:

The Love of the Beloved is like unto fire,
And understanding warps it like smoke,
As flows the flame of love, smoke melts away.[1]

Farid tells us that reason or understanding dispels the fire of
love. Love burns in the fire of longing and not from reason or
intellectual disputation. Hazur Baba Sawan Singh went so far as
to say that "we should throw hundreds of books into the fire if
necessary, for our hearts should be a garden of the flowers of
love."[2]

The point is that outer knowledge at this point stands in
contradiction to the truths of love. Reason is a faculty of the
mind and not an aspect of the essence of love. Whoever is not
prepared to renounce speculative reasoning will never enter
the abode of love. Meher Baba, the Indian avatar, would often
caution his disciples that "no amount of intellect can take us to
God. No amount of austerity can enable us to attain God. It is
only when we love Him and lose ourselves in Him that we attain to unity. It is only by the feat of love that we lose ourselves,
that the two become one."

The lover who would proceed farther along this avenue-
must abandon the baggage of "perception" and discursive
reasoning. Unquestioning obedience to the Beloved is not
attainable until intellectual judgment is withheld. Judgment is
the last stronghold of the intellect. But God cannot be
fathomed, nor can His ways be intellectually understood.
Submission to the will of the Beloved is submission to the
slavery and dominance of love. How can the hand of freedom
ever touch the skirt of the lover? Such "freedom" would imply
the loss of the Beloved.

Expansion of the Heart

When we abandon the attempt to use our minds to appre-
hend God, we see the world for the first time without the dis-
torting spectacles of thought. Suddenly the world seems vastly
more immediate and powerful than the lover ever imagined.
Saint John of the Cross tells us:

At times a man wonders if he is being charmed and he goes about with wonderment over what he sees and hears. Everything seems so very strange even though he is the same person as always. The reason is he is being made a stranger to his usual knowledge and experience of things.[3]

The process of becoming a stranger to the known rearranges the lover's perception of the world. Farid Attar uses metaphor to describe the immensity of this spiritual change that occurs:

In this state of the soul a cold wind blows, so violent that in a moment it devastates an immense space; the seven oceans are no more than a pool, the seven planets a mere spark, the seven heavens a corpse, the seven hells broken ice. Then an astonishing thing, beyond reason, an ant has the strength of a hundred elephants, and a hundred caravans perish while a rook is filling his crop.[4]

Here Attar is speaking of a love that discovers the infinite power of its own self-sufficiency, while simultaneously realizing that this creative power is reduced to powder in the presence of the supreme love. We use here the word "violent," because as Attar so graphically explains, all normal phenomena are disturbed. The entire emotional makeup of the personality of the lover goes through a deep metamorphosis.

At this station, the lover's ideas of the Beloved also undergo a significant change. The lover realizes that the person of the mentor or Beloved has, in reality, nothing to do with the essence of love. The physical form is merely the steed of the Beloved. It is not its commander. The real form of the Beloved is love, uncreated light, or as it is referred to in the New Testament "the Word made flesh."

In the mature state of love, the lover will see no "otherness" in the being of the Beloved. The Beloved is the perfect manifestation of God's plenty; the perfect vehicle for the transmission of God's will. The nameless absolute dwells in the "Word made flesh." Jesus said (John 12:49):

For I have not spoken on my authority.
The Father Who has sent me

has Himself given me commandment
what to say and what to speak.

Guarding the Heart

There is a wonderful story that illustrates the dilemma of the intellect unable to submit to the will of the Beloved.

Lord Krishna remarked that he had a pain in His stomach, the cure of which could only be effected by the heart of a living person. He told one of His closest devotees to get such a heart from somewhere; otherwise He would die. The devotee was so concerned that he ran at once and began searching from house to house, but no one was willing to cut his or her heart out and give it.

All day he searched, until finally at night, exhausted and desperate, he came to the home of a prostitute. When he told her of his mission, she said, "All right, here, take it," and thereupon cut out her heart and handed it to him. The devotee ran with the heart to Lord Krishna and sank at His feet. Lord Krishna said, "Oh, you finally found one person who loved me enough to give her heart! But what about yourself? Are you not supposed to be my closest devotee? Are you not a human with a heart as well?"

When we speak about "violent love," we imply a state that transcends the dualities of life and death. For the lover, mad with love for the Beloved, nothing is impossible, and nothing inevitable. The will of the Beloved is the very life of the lover.

There is a remarkably similar story from the history of the Sikhs that illustrates the ease with which a true lover offers himself or herself in the service of the Beloved. During the violent and cruel reign of the Mughvals, who tried by force of the sword to convert the Sikhs to Islam, Guru Arjan called upon the brethren to resist all attempts at forced conversion.

It so happened that on one occasion the Master, seeking to test the faith and obedience of the disciples, asked for a volunteer against whose body he could test one of his rifles. At his request, not one but two disciples jumped forth, vying to be the first to test the rifle. The youngest among them stepped forth and pleaded with the guru that the others had already tasted the gift of surrender to the Beloved, but he was young and should now be given this opportunity.

The second and elder Sikh pleaded that the younger one would have many more times to offer his life in the service of the Master but that he was old and should be permitted to die in honor. The guru, knowing the inner condition of both, fired two shots from his rifle. One bullet hit the younger, and the other hit the older of the two. In that instant both were spiritually transformed and the glow of illumination shone from their faces.

These stories, which may appear fanciful at first reading, illustrate the love that can obey with reckless disregard of world and self. "Which of you," the Bible asks, "by taking thought can add one cubit to his stature?" When reasoning and understanding have been displaced by the transcendent and supremely harmonizing force of love, the heart expands, realizing its own connectedness to everything that it perceives. Reason is one of the most opaque veils separating us from the face of the Beloved.

Absolute Secrecy

In the last phase of this corridor of violent love, the lover is required to maintain absolute secrecy with regard to the condition of his or her heart. Love is a secret, not only because it arises from the pre-temporal domain, but because words mar the sublimity of its perfection. One mystic wrote, "Love is covered and no one has ever seen it revealed."

The lover, then, despite all agonies, reveals nothing of his or her love to the world. It is a state that cannot be described, since love, like God, is only fully revealed in the pre-temporal grandeur of love. In the realm of temporality, love must be concealed, for its very nature cannot be fully experienced in the realm of time. How, then, can it possibly be explained or understood via words?

Those who speak the language of love speak it without words. The problem here, as Sant Darshan Singh has explained, is that "the lover can neither explain his inner condition nor keep it entirely from the view of others. The path of love is as slippery as a razor's edge. Hence, any outward display of our intoxication, our love for the Master, may uncover a certain pride. It may lead to the expression, however subtle, of the ego although it is hiding behind the veil of enthusiasm. In any outward show of our bliss, elation, or ecstasy, it is essential to make sure that there is not the least semblance of pride. Otherwise, the intoxication will wither away in no time."[5] In contradiction to the Western model, where it is quite in order for the lover to display his or her love, mystic love in the East is always a silent yearning, a silent burning, and nobody is supposed to know about it. One of Sant Darshan Singh's verses captures this thought eloquently:

> *The blood of my desires has been shed a thousand times.*
> *But nobody has ever seen even a tear in my eye.*
> *I have borne all atrocities, all eccentricities,*
> *All idiosyncrasies, all sorts of torture and indifference,*
> *for the sake of my Beloved;*
> *Yet I have never complained.*[6]

Even the very stars and flowers are to be kept from the secrets of love. The bird of love does not alight upon the tarnished flowers of the world but within the heart of one whose love is like an invisible cool breeze in the midst of the heat of the world. According to the principles of love, even tears are a blemish, for tears are an expression of love that has already lost its dignity.

In yet another verse Sant Darshan explains the loss of honor that a lover undergoes when his or her tears become a "visible display of love":

> *The moment the molten heart*
> *can be seen in the form of tears,*
> *Our love no longer remains a secret;*
> *It loses its sublimity.*[7]

This betrayal of the eyes is a great loss of honor for the lover, because love is a secret and must remain a secret. For Westerners this concept of secrecy may at first seem strange, for why indeed should one conceal such a wonderful state of love?

There are several reasons for this concealment. In the first place, as we have mentioned, there can be no adequate description of the lover's relationship to the Beloved. To attempt to describe it is to demean it. Its sublimity is its beauty. By speaking, the lover asserts his or her own individuality. Any assertion on the part of the lover is considered a sign of spiritual immaturity and a sacrilege. One cannot assert one's own love, only the love of the Beloved. Yet the difficulty of this stage is that it is also not possible to completely hide the secret of one's love within oneself. A gnostic explains this unique predicament when he says:

> *However much I may conceal*
> *the pang of my love for thee,*
> *My foolish tears betray me.*
> *My pale face betokens my inability*
> *to bear separation from thee.*
> *It throws into open the secret hidden in me.*[8]

Jesus cautioned his followers on a number of occasions against flaunting their good works. He admonished them to "do thy good works in secret. And thy Father, who seeth that which is hidden, shall reward thee openly."

The lover who completes this phase of concealment moves forward with the jewel of the Beloved hidden within the deepest recesses of his or her heart. Unable to express anything of his or her love, the lover walks the path of self-abandonment and humility.

Following page:
Moses and the Burning Bush and Moses Receiving the Law
Conde Museum, Chantilly

In this illumination from a Danish Psalter, Moses hears God speaking to him from a burning bush. The bush represents the lover's own physical form, here shown surrounded by other aspects of the physical world. While the lover may in the early stages perceive the Divine Beloved as exterior to himself or herself, as Moses does here, he or she is drawn irresistibly into unity and eventually merges with the Beloved. The second illustration depicts Moses receiving the tablets containing the Law from God on Mount Sinai.

The Three Faces of Blame

O men of lust, beware of entering
this land of love.
Here you will find only
the cross and the gallows.

—Sant Darshan Singh.

It is said that once a princess named Zaibul-Nisa went to Sarmad, a Jewish saint of the seventeenth century, and requested of him the rare boon of God's love. Sarmad replied:

O friends, the burning passion for the Lord
is not granted to the avaricious,
nor the moth's love for the flame
to flies that hover 'round filth.
It takes ages to get the revelation of the Lord.
This wealth is not doled out
to all and sundry.[1]

The path to inner purification, as Sarmad pointed out, is not lined with roses. For the lover, the struggle for inner unification is a path of great sacrifice and trial. All passions must gradually be subdued and in their stead one sole passion remains: love for the Beloved. It is not, then, simply sexual love that must be mastered, but anything at all that may come between the lover and the Beloved. Sensual love is but one aspect of the Hydra-headed face of desire.

For the lover, three distinct aspects emerge in the perfection of love. The Sufis have referred to these as *the three faces of blame*. These "faces" are turned, one toward the world of creation, one toward the lover, and one toward the Beloved.

Farid Attar explains that the "face toward the world of creation is the sword of the Beloved's jealousy; it consists in keeping the lover from paying attention to anything other than the Beloved. The face toward the lover is the sword of time's jealousy and it consists in keeping the lover from paying attention to himself or herself. Finally, the face towards the Beloved is the sword of love's jealousy; it consists in making the lover take nourishment from nothing but love, and in compelling himself or herself to seek nothing from outside [love's essence]."[2]

These three "faces" are the means by which the lover severs himself or herself from all things other than love, even if it be the Beloved. For even the Beloved may function as something "other." As we can readily see, the lover during this phase, and indeed throughout the journey, is engaged in a continual process of assertion and negation: assertion, in that he or she asserts only the existence and reality of love, and negation in that he or she negates all aspects of "otherness" in him- or herself.

When Sant Darshan invites lovers to the cross and the gallows, this is part of the process of negation. Desire is the movement of the soul away from the Beloved, for in the perfect state nothing is allowed in the sanctuary of love except love itself. The poet has summed up this perfection of love:

> *I would be disloyal*
> *and could not claim to be in love with you.*
> *If I ever cried for your help,*
> *You may impose union or separation,*
> *I am untouched by these two,*
> *your love is enough for me.*[3]

Blame toward Oneself

The first face of blame requires the lover to transcend the influence of the five outer senses, which are reflected in the major vices: lust, greed, attachment, avarice, and jealousy. In this phase the physical plane is transcended and the elixir of the Beloved's glances within replaces attachment to outer enjoyments. The lover still may not be free from subtle reflections of these attachments on the inner planes, for that is not fully accomplished until much later stages. However, the veil has been drawn aside within, and the lover begins to subsist on the inner radiant form of the Beloved. The centering of the lover's attention in the radiant form of the Master reflects not only the ability to absent himself or herself from creation but an attunement to the essence of Love.

Blame toward the World

During the second phase of blame or renunciation of self, the lover is called upon to utterly deny himself or herself. In this process the five inner senses and their attachments to inner phenomena are transcended. Here the ego finds nowhere to hide and comes against the full force of love. Here the lover acknowledges the essential illusory nature of his or her ego, the source of all "I-ness," evidenced by pride, egotism, vanity, and the drive to accomplish. We have ample testimony to this thought in both Hindu and Judaic-Christian traditions, in *The Imitation of Christ,*: "If thou wilt be my disciple, deny thyself utterly."[4] And in the language of the great non-dualist Ramana Maharshi:

> *Renunciation is non-identification of the self*
> *With the non-self.*[5]

The paradoxical nature of renunciation is revealed succinctly in the Tao Te Ching (XXII), in which it is said:

> *He who has little will receive*
> *He who has much will be embarrassed.*

To understand this process it may be helpful to perceive the lover as gradually divesting himself or herself of all the shackles of "phenomena" first, and then of "nomena." This peeling away of the self reverses the process of perception itself. The divesting of mind, or *manas*, the emotions, the intellect, or *buddhi*, and in the later stages ego, or *ahankar* (the root cause of individuality), proceeds in direct proportion to the interiorization of love.

Blame toward the Beloved

The last phase of this journey through "otherness" is reflected in the third face of blame, directed toward the Beloved. It is at this phase that even the Beloved may act as something "other" and become an obstacle to the lover's realization of the ultimate essence of Love. So long as the Beloved is perceived as *other than* love, as other than oneself, as other than the God Supreme, the reality of union is not possible.

There is a story in the *Mahabarata* that aptly describes this sense of otherness with regard to the Beloved. It is said that once Krishna went on a tour to Benares, about one hundred miles from Brindavan. Although Udho pleaded with Krishna to take him along with him, he instructed Udho to remain behind. For nearly two weeks Udho was languishing in a state of separation, shedding copious tears all the while. Krishna neither appeared in his meditations nor returned from his tour. Finally, after nearly two weeks, Krishna appeared to him. Udho despairingly asked why had it taken so long for him to appear.

Krishna replied, "Had you thought I was the life of your life and the breath of your breath, I would have appeared instantly, but since you thought I resided in Benares, it took me two weeks to get here by the road."

The Beloved is not simply a form that appears within, but the supreme center of the universe, the supreme center of our own existence. At this stage, the lover realizes there are no limitations to the infiniteness of the Beloved. It was to this reality that the Persian mystic Shabistari alluded when he said,

In all things,
See but One, say but One, know One.[6]

Or in the words of the contemporary woman Saint Ananda Moyi Ma:

The inward and the outward are indissolubly united
and form a single great eternal current.[7]

Or again in the words of Hermes:

Not that the One is Two,
but that these two are one.
The One is neither I nor thou, this nor that.

Rumi personified that quest for love in every fiber of his being. For Rumi, the Beloved is not found or sought nor even "become," but that essence in which we drown without our own awareness. In fact, the world itself is not other than love; it is merely the veil of forgetfulness, which instantly dissolves when the Beloved is recognized. Rumi writes:

Seek him in the placeless, he will sign you to a place.
When you seek him in the place,
he will flee to the placeless.
As the arrow speeds from the bow,
like the bird of your imagination.
Know that the Absolute
will certainly flee from the Imaginary.[8]

Rumi says emphatically that there is no place where the Beloved is not. One cannot seek Him anywhere, for thought itself flees from the Beloved. The realm of desire will always flee from the realm of illumination, and illumination from that of desire. So too does the Beloved flee from every aspect of "otherness," which is only the shadow of the real. The real is not and cannot be sought by an act of will, imagination, or thought, but is who we are when illusion is removed. It is this realization that is the essence of unity.

Sri Aurobindo gives us an indication of the experience of unity when he discusses his own condition:

One begins to feel others too as part of oneself or varied
repetitions of oneself, the same self modified by Nature in

*other bodies. Or, at the least, as living in the larger univer-
sal self which is henceforth one's own greater reality. All
things in fact begin to change their nature and appearance;
one's whole experience of the world is radically different
from that of those who are shut up in their personal selves.
One begins to know things by a different kind of experience,
more direct, not depending on the external mind and
senses. It is not that the possibility of error disappears, for
that cannot be so long as mind of any kind is one's instrument for transcribing knowledge, but there is a new, vast
and deep way of experiencing, seeing, knowing, contacting
things; and the confines of knowledge can be rolled back to
an almost unmeasurable degree.*[9]

Following page:
Rosette Bearing the Name & Titles of Emperor Shah Jahan
Metropolitan Museum of Art, New York

The mandala, in both Sufi and Hindu iconography, is a reflection of both the cosmos and the cosmic process. The following example is a Mughval work ca. 1645. It represents all things moving in perfect symmetry from the Absolute Unity through its theophany back to Unity. To the mystic encamped in the palace of Unity, the mandala reflects the surrender of the self and the reintegration of the many into the One. Here the mystic becomes a being of true insight and, holding up the cup of divinity, sees all things as if through a glass clearly.

The Unity of Essence

Take all humanity in thy loving embrace
For they are thine own kith and kin.
And go thy way distributing love
To all who walk the streets

—Sant Darshan Singh

The words of Sant Darshan above are the echo that resounds at the door of unity. Anyone who passes through that door speaks with the same tongue. Part becomes whole, or as Farid Attar more perfectly remarks, "there will be neither part nor whole; the Being I speak of does not exist separately; everyone is this Being, existence and non-existence. Everything is perishing except His Face, unless thou art in His Face [essence] do not seek to exist. Whoever is uttering 'I' and 'we' at the door, he is turned back from the door."[1]

When the lover sees none but the Friend, and Him alone, then, as Abdul Al Qudiri Jilani, the great Sufi of Baghdad, says, "We have passed by ourselves and cut asunder all other ties."[2] In Christian terms, this move toward the universal unity has been described as the entering of the Son into the infinite Being, so that even Sonship is subject to the absoluteness of God. In First Corinthians (15:28) it is explained,

And when all things shall be subdued unto him,
then shall the son also himself be subject unto him
that put all things under him,
That God may be all in all.

In a similar vein we hear from a Jewish mystic who paints a picture of unity that much resembles the Hindu ideal of of the sense of unity Radha feels gazing upon her Beloved Krishna.

O Lord of the universe
I will sing thee a sound.
Where canst Thou be found?
And where canst Thou not be found?
Where I pass—there art Thou.
Thou, Thou and only Thou.
Thou are, Thou hast been and Thou wilt be.
Thou didst reign, Thou reignest, and Thou wilt reign.
Thine is Heaven, Thine is Earth,
Thou fillest high regions,
And Thou fillest low regions.
Wheresoever I turn Thou, Oh, Thou art there[3]

Unity Consciousness

The recognition of this unity is the quintessence of all revealed spiritual traditions. To the lover, the realization of unity comes in degrees during the various stages he or she passes through. The first step is the recognition of the Beloved in all, in which the Divine Beloved becomes the repository of all existence. Krishna tells Arjuna on the battlefield of this state, "Whoever sees me in all, and all creation in me, he is my Beloved. The clay is the same, formed into different shapes by the Potter; all the same, they are clay with conscious entity residing therein."

The second step toward the consciousness of unity is the recognition of the self-sameness of that Beloved to oneself. No longer is the Beloved other than oneself. In the Hindu scripture, the Chandogya Upanishad Brahamana, it says, "That which is the finest essence—this whole world has that as its Self. That is Reality. That is Atman [Supreme Self]. That art thou, Svetaketu."[4] The Lankavatara Sutra reaffirms the same reality: "Self-realization is based on identity and oneness."[5] But to enter into it the disciple must be free from all presuppositions and attachments to things.

Cessation of Desire

One of the most memorable extracts from the Buddhist text, the *Dhammapada*, is the Buddha's Victory Song. It describes the dismantling of the superstructure of illusion and ego. Buddha describes each lifetime as a house built by God. These houses or lifetimes are made necessary by the soul's desires. Of the cessation of such desire, Buddha says:

Seeking the builder of the house,
I have run my course in the vortex
Of countless births, never escaping
the hobble of death:
Ill is repeated birth after birth.
Householder, thou art seen!
Never again shalt thou build me a house.

All of thy rigging is broken,
The peak of the roof is shattered;
Its aggregations passed away,
Mind has reached the destruction of cravings.[6]

Desire ceases when we realize our own divine perfection, own Buddha nature. We realize that we ourselves are the Beloved that we have been seeking. Distinctions fade away. When the ego dies there is only love, neither Beloved nor lover, both of which are aspects of a conditioned existence. It is desire or craving that creates conditions, and their removal shatters illusory existence. The Vedanta scriptures say, "the Self is Brahman."

Unity expresses itself in concrete form in the outer world as action that exhibits no personal interest or motivation for selfish ends. When we read of the selfless acts of the great saints and Masters, we often wonder how anyone can act with such total personal disregard. Yet the vision of the unity of essence precludes any other type of action. The love that has transcended its own self-interest cannot fail to express a unitive and life-affirming ethos. Here, it is not what one does that is important, but the quality of love that is manifest in those actions. The experience of selfless love, which began as a gift from the Beloved, is now channeled back to all creation.

There is an exquisite story that describes this.

During the Mughval reign in India, the Muslim rulers tried repeatedly to forcibly convert the Sikhs to Islam at swordpoint. Sikh history is replete with martyrs of love, but one man, Bhai Kaneya, stands out as unique in this respect.

During one of the many battles waged against one small band of Sikhs who resisted, it was noticed that Bhai Kaneya, who was in charge of giving water to the wounded, was giving water not only to the wounded Sikhs but also to the Muslims who had fallen in battle. He was accused by the other Sikhs of high treason.

After much debate, the case was brought before Guru Arjan Dev, the spiritual leader of the Sikh faith at the time, and a perfect Master as well. It was explained to him that Bhai Kaneya was hindering the Sikhs from winning the war for their religious freedom by reviving the enemy's wounded at the very moment when they needed it most.

Arjan Dev heard the accusations in a quiet and pensive mood, knowing all the while the real state of his disciples. Then he asked Bhai Kaneya to respond to the allegations against him. Bhai Kaneya, in his usual gentle manner, said, "Sir, I give water neither to the Muslims nor to the Sikhs, I give water to you and you alone. Wherever I see your effluent light I pay my obeisance. Wherever I see your radiant face I give water to you."

The guru replied, "This is the only man who has truly understood my teachings. And from now on Bhai Kaneya will not only give water to the Sikhs and Muslims, but he will balm and bandage them as well."

Perfection of Outer Conduct

During this stage, as the story of Bhai Kaneya illustrates so well, the lover perfects his or her conduct in the world. The true lover now views everything as an aspect of the essence of love and therefore makes no distinction between enemy and friend, good and bad, right and wrong. When the awakened soul pierces beyond the veil to the noetic and unitive vision, he or she witnesses all forms embedded in one reality.

Every atom of the universe pulsates in the divine essence of love. The true lover harmonizes with every being because he or she experiences them as himself or herself. His or her experience is always inclusive of others, never exclusive. True compassion, like that of Bhai Kaneya, arises because there is no room for distinction or diversion.

Ramakrishna Param-hansa, in trying to describe this state, once said that "it was like seeing every form wrapped in a silken cloth of light. The forms themselves were there but they were of a dream-like quality. Each form, whether an ant or an elephant, was the Supreme Reality."

The direct result of this state is the transformation of the outer personality and the perfection of virtues. The lover swims in the ocean of equanimity and compassion while serving others selflessly. The lover who experiences this realization becomes a person of true insight. Things do not happen *to* him or her but *in* him or her. The divisions between inner and outer disappear. Whatever is happening, is happening in and through the cosmic body. In this state, the lover eats through the mouths of others, sees through the eyes of others, and feels through the heart of others. Service to others is found to be service to the one Beloved. What else can the lover do now except serve the light that he or she is?

Mother Teresa of Calcutta was once asked, "Mother, how does it happen you are able to do so much, and why are you in this state of joy?"

"My dear," she said, "it is because I am so deeply in love."

"But, Mother, you're a nun,"

"Precisely," she said. "I am married to Jesus."

"Yes, I understand, you're married to Jesus. All nuns are."

"No, you don't understand," she countered. "I really am so in a state of love that I see the face of my Beloved in the face of the dying man in the streets of Calcutta. I see my Beloved in the day-old child who's left outside our convent, and in the leper whose flesh is decaying; and I can't do enough for my Beloved! That is why I try to do something beautiful for God."[7]

All in One and One in All

This sacred vision of the All in One and the One in All, which Mother Teresa so beautifully describes, is an act of supreme self-surrender. This vision is not static but dynamic, and compels the lover to act as any lover would in the service of his or her Beloved. Wherever the lover sees the Beloved, he or she is called to action. The lover is committed to the service of all humanity, for that very service is an act of love to the Beloved.

This outward action of the lover is not something that occurs only at one stage; it occurs from the very beginning of the search for the Beloved. But what is unique to this particular stage is its grounding in ecstatic *vision*.

When serving the Beloved, in whatever form that service may take, the lover no longer notices any difference between the Beloved and his or her own most interior self. So who is serving whom? For his or her actions to be described as "service" is astonishing to the lover, for there is no recollection except of love. The great Zen Masters have tried in, their own unique way, to explain this mystery. The poet-monk Sengtsan alludes to this:

> In the World of Reality there is no self,
> There is no other-than-self.[8]

It is this mystery that is at the back of the lover's bewilderment, for concepts are meaningless in a state of love. When the lover is charged with this self-effacing love, the power of love is present in a sacred, ever-deepening, ever-widening sphere of love. Everyone the lover meets is empowered and connected to that same cosmic fire of love that consumes everything except the Beloved.

It is not accidental that this chapter appears at this point in the lover's evolution toward total unity. The lover is entering into the causal or noetic plane of the universe, in which the basic building blocks of the universe are revealed. Here the outer qualities of the lover begin to disappear. If he or she was a contemplative, he or she no longer remains one; if he or she was a lover, he or she is now without a Beloved. Whatever quality he or she had is now lost to him or her. Attar says of this state that the lover "has been reduced to nothing in Thee."[9]

This transcendence of relative values and ethics is indeed a difficult task, for it involves the dismantling of the subtlest aspects of desire. The primary quality that supports personality in illusion is ego. And therefore whatever we most pride ourselves in is shattered. This is not ordinary suffering, but transpersonal, for we are not speaking about the outer garments of personality as it is seen by others, but the very fabric of consciousness itself. Here the entire storehouse of karmic effects, going back countless ages, is rent asunder, and the knot between the conscious life-force *(shakti)* and the unconscious *(prakriti)* is untied for good. It is as if the mirror in which perception itself is perceived is shattered.

A lively Hindu folk song to Kali, the symbol of the destroyer, epitomizes this stage:

Confoundress with Thy Flashing sword,
Thoughtlessly Thou has put to death
my virtue and my sin alike.[10]

It is manifestation itself that is rooted out, to be replaced with "Pure existence [which] is beyond cause and effect." And pure existence is pure and perfect love.

Following page:
Mohammed's Night Journey
Metropolitan Museum of Art, New York

The Night Journey of Mohammed represented in this illuminated manuscript culminates in his reaching the seventh heaven (top of the causal plane). Here, enveloped in a golden cloud, he bows before the Throne of Allah in an ecstasy approaching annihilation. The Almighty communicates to him ninety-nine ineffable words of the Law and commandments.

Ecstasy

What does it matter if we never regain our senses?
This day O Cupbearer, pour forth as much as we can drink.
—Sant Darshan Singh

If the lover is fortunate enough to reach this station, he or she becomes a true citizen of the realm of love. Having rent asunder the veils of intellect and reason, the lover quaffs the cup of ecstasy and comes to the fountain-head of the primal source of creation. During this most marvelous station, four movements are articulated as the lover journeys forth.

First, the Beloved *reveals* to the world the inner condition of the lover's heart. The coveted secret of love between the Beloved and the lover becomes an open book for all to see. In the second phase, the lover passes beyond *self-awareness* and discernment, rejection, or acceptance. In the third phase, the lover plunges into the *sea of intoxication*, never to see the shores of his or her existence again.

In the final phase of ecstasy, the lover is reduced to *total poverty* of the spirit. There is not the least concern whether he or she is accepted or rejected, whether he or she is in union or separation. In this beguiling condition when the lover meets the Beloved, he or she will "disappear" in direct proportion to the maturity of his or her love. The lover has become, as a human individual, completely transparent.

Immersed in the rapturous inner light and music, Kabir explains the wonder of the thunderous sound of the sacred Om as it resounds throughout all creation:

> *Think of it, knower of Brahma*
> *It's pouring, pouring, the thunder's roaring,*
> *But not one rain drop falls.*

Revealing the Lover's Heart

In the first phase, which the Sufis have called *ishitar*, the Beloved gives full publicity to the inner condition of the lover's heart. The lover, however, has become so immersed in the ecstasy of his or her love that he or she cares for neither the respect nor the disapproval of the world. The Beloved, however, in seeking to test the purity and steadfastness of his or her condition, sets a clever trap for the lover. The trap consists in revealing to others the perfection of the lover's inner attainment. The lover, left to his or her own, would not dare to reveal this secret love before the multitudes. The lover's desire is to remain concealed from the world, which would in the end only create distraction.

At this point, many difficulties may arise that cause great agitation, turmoil, and anguish. The lover may find the bait of the world's attention too much to bear, and succumb to worldly adulation and praise. Yet, if the lover remains steadfast, he or she remains unaffected by the adulation and praise of others, instead diving still deeper into the ecstasy of his or her own heart.

There is in fact a whole tradition in Christian hagiography that documents the lovers of God as *fools of Christ*, who commit extravagant acts in an attempt to hide themselves from the eyes of the world. There is a similar tradition in Islam among those known as *malamatiyah*, or "the people of blame," who strive for the same end. In India, too, there has always been a tradition of the fierce or mad *must* who may at times violently abuse people in order to preserve his or her privacy. The mystic poet Hafiz had this in mind when composing this *ghazal:*

The world exalts the base, denies the lordly soul repose.
For from the palate of the sense wash off, O heart,
The taste for greed or cov'tous deed.
Go far away from lips of eager hope,
From tongue of longing deep,
Their sweet or bitter deep,
O Haste, bring us wine
And drown in wine the sham insulting lures of boors.[1]

During this phase, the lover's love is crystallized into something sublime and permanent. No longer fearful of outward distractions, the lover now moves inward, united with, and in remembrance of, the Beloved. Here the inner vision of the lover is opened and the secrets of eternity can be read like an open book.

It is here that reason is truly sunk as it is immersed in a sea of "pure witnessing." Kabir, with his characteristic simplicity, put it this way:

Nectar in a Bundle
I took it down from my head.
When I tell them it's one
They say two and four instead.[2]

Oblivion

In the second phase of this process of ecstasy, the lover not only loses all sense and sensibility in an ordinary context, but also becomes *oblivious to his or her own condition* and ultimately even to his or her own ecstasy.

During this process the lover is neither an ascetic nor a *sadhu*, neither of this world nor of the next world. The lover is *aware solely of not being aware.* The consciousness of the lover is almost destroyed in the process of witnessing the Beloved's beauty. Yet the lover retains just enough individuality to taste of the bliss of this wondrous state. The lover becomes reckless to attain the final consummation of union, and now "charges forth like one drunk and finds his or her way to the *Kharabat*, or tavern of love." Matilda of Magdeburg, an early Christian saint, spoke knowingly of this wine and of its potent charms, which render the lover "poor and naked":

> *Wouldst thou come with me to the wine cellar?*
> *That will cost thee much:*
> *Even hadst thou a thousand marks*
> *It were all spent in one hour.*
> *If thou wouldst drink the unmingled wine*
> *Thou must ever spend more than thou hast,*
> *And the Host will never fill thy glass to the brim.*
> *Thou wilt become poor and naked,*
> *Despised of all who would rather see themselves in the dust*
> *Than squander their all in the wine cellar.*[3]

As Matilda colorfully states, this divine inebriation leaves the lover stripped of all that he or she took to be himself or herself. What remains is the majesty of ecstasy. In a more analytical vein, the mystics tell us that the physical body, composed of five elements (earth, water, fire, air, and ether); the subtle body, consisting of seventeen elements (five organs of perception: eyes, nose, ears, mouth, and skin; five of action: sight, hearing, smell, taste, and touch; the five vital airs, and *manas* and *buddhi*) has been peeled back, as it were, from the self-luminous consciousness that is love. What then remains is the last of the five coverings, called by Advaitism the *anandmai* (bliss) covering, which is none other than the *self-consciousness* of one's own bliss. This bliss is a reflection of the infinite bliss of the perfect nature of love. It is the reflection of love viewed in the mirror of the lover's mind.

Acceptance and Rejection

If the Beloved favors the lover and he or she endures this favor without losing sight of the Beloved, he or she gains the state described in the Qur'an (53:17): "His sight never swerved nor did it go wrong." In this state only the slightest thread of ego remains to prevent the lover from realizing his or her complete identity with love itself.

It is at this point that the lover enters into what the Sufis have called *kahf*, the cave of union.[4] In this cave the poor helpless lover goes mad with love for the Beloved. During this madness of love, the lover has not the slightest concern for whether he or she is accepted or rejected, whether he or she lives or dies. As one poet said:

> *If a thousand lashes of "By no means canst thou see Me direct" are lashed upon the lover's back, even then the lover will go reiterating the cry: "Show thy Face to me that I may behold Thee." Even in the face of the totally impossible, the lover cries out, "It is possible!"*[5]

The Sea of Intoxication

Under the spell of this wine, the entire reality of the lover is turned upside down. Saint Isaac of Syria, one of the early Christian fathers, seems to have spoken to this point:

> *Love for God is naturally ardent and when it fills a man to overflowing, leads the soul to ecstasy. Therefore, the heart of a man who experiences it cannot bear it, but undergoes an extraordinary change according to its own quality and the quality of the love which fills him. He is as one out of his mind. A terrible death is for him a joy, and his mental contemplation of heavenly things is never broken.*[6]

In this state of divine ecstasy, the lover's experience is so profound that there is nothing that can divert his or her attention from the Beloved. Al Ghazzali reveals to what extent this madness takes hold of the lover:

> *Even if the gnostic were cast into the fire,*
> *he would not feel it, because of his absorption,*
> *and if the delights of paradise were spread out before him,*
> *he would not turn toward them,*
> *because of the perfection of the grace that is in him,*
> *and his perfect attainment,*
> *which is above all else that can be attained.*[7]

In this elevated state of primordial witnessing, the soul remains immersed in the rapturous strains of divine light and inner music. The brilliance and magnitude of this light is such that the lover perceives nothing but his or her own bliss and

light. Richard of Saint Victor, a little-known Christian mystic of
the Middle Ages, described this predicament when he said:

*For when the mind of man is carried beyond itself
all the limits of human reasoning are overpassed.
For the whole system of human suffering and reasoning
succumbs to that
which the soul perceives of the divine light,
when she is raised above herself
and ravished in ecstasy.*[8]

In the Song of Solomon (7:9), we have a reference to a state
of ecstasy that is beyond rational communication. This vision
of light is compared to

*Wine that goeth down sweetly,
causing the lips of those that are asleep to speak
and those who are awake to fall to dead silence.*

In much of Eastern literature, and in particular Sufi poetry,
the light that emanates from the *Murshid*, or guide, is referred
to as the wine in the tavern of God. It is the God-man or
Murshid who dispenses this wine, which proceeds directly
from the "flagon" of the Master's eyes to the various disciples,
or "tipplers." It was this wine which Omar Khayyam immortalized in his *Rubaiyat:*

*You know, my friends, with what a brave carouse,
I made a Second Marriage in my house;
Divorced old barren Reason from my Bed,
And took the Daughter of the Vine to Spouse.*[9]

The Spanish poet and mystic Nablusi, an early medieval
saint, speaks of this divine intoxicant as well:

*Wine signifies the drink of divine love, which results from
contemplating the traces of His beautiful names [His at-
tributes]. For this love begets drunkenness and the complete
forgetfulness of all that exists in the world.*[10]

In such a state, there is nothing left but the Beloved. Khwaja Hafiz spoke as one who would gladly forsake all for the Divine Friend:

None finds room in my heart save my Friend.
O Lord, give both the worlds to my adversaries,
My Friend is enough for me.[11]

Sant Darshan Singh uses remarkably similar language, though writing in the twentieth century in India:

Look at the overcast sky unburdening itself, O love,
Spill forth thy wine in a like measure, O love,
And let the wine of Oneness so overwhelm us, O love,
That all distinctions and divisions be lost, O love,
Thy divine vintage has at last cleansed me, O love,
Now unfold the mystery of the two worlds, O love.[12]

It is unfortunate that many Western readers are unaware of the subtle psychological and spiritual implications hidden within the verses of many Sufi, Christian and Hindu mystics as well as those from other traditions. Their verses, as we have seen, are only "the adornment of a Sufi's dress, they do not even touch the threshold of knowledge."

Words cannot express the intense intoxication that the lover experiences at this stage, when even the tiniest drop of that wine is "a hundred times more wonderful than any sensual enjoyment."[13] Still, with all this, the door of perfect love has not been opened. The test of this truth comes when the lover, in the act of seeing the physical form of the Beloved "becomes agitated." This is because "his existence is provisionally borrowed and he faces non-existence. In the ecstasy of love *(wajd)* his existence is agitated, until he rests with the reality of love."[14]

As this love perfects itself, the lover looks so deep into the heart of love that he or she looks nowhere but within for the source of his or her nourishment. Marsilo Fecino, a Christian saint, indicates this state when he speaks about the perfect contemplation in "which we become that very happiness itself."[15]

Thus, as the luminosity of love descends into the heart of the lover, the intellect (which is merely another covering of the soul) is discarded and true ecstasy manifests itself in direct proportion to its displacement. Sant Darshan Singh suggests to lovers the greatness of this love when he says:

> *Oh tell the darkness of intellect*
> *To seek the madness of love,*
> *For this madness is a beam of light,*
> *And nothing but light.*[16]

Fellowship with the Friend is unfortunately another dream of the imagination, because the lover can never become truly intimate with the Beloved. So long as the lover remains, the Beloved hides His face from the court of union. What we have become we can no longer experience as "other."[17] Paradoxically, then, even ecstasy must be obliterated, because it is contingent upon or nourished by the state of separation. The lover, realizing his or her condition of ecstasy is predicated upon separate existence, must decide between tasting the honey or becoming it. If the lover is fortunate he or she plunges headlong into the sea of martyrdom and becomes the honey itself.

Some Eastern mystics refer to a final step in love in which the breath of the lover may acquire both the scent (jasmine) and the color of the Beloved, or the lover may even exchange physical forms with the Beloved. As the Beloved opens His heart in a gesture of final acceptance, the lover loses all awareness of even the slightest aspect of himself or herself.

Following page:
The Ascent into the Empyrean
Metropolitan Museum of Art, New York

In this painting by Hieronymus Bosch (1450-1516), the soul reaches the end of the long journey and approaches the Ultimate, naked and alone. Pregnant with divine longing, the lover faces the perfect effulgence of God, which both encompasses and permeates the entire universe.

CHAPTER

The Disappearance of Reality

Through martyrdom alone,
One reaches the destination.
My life is but the dust of the martyrs.

—Sant Darshan Singh

During this most baffling and perplexing station of the journey, the lover finds himself or herself in a field of paradoxes. This stage is also traditionally characterized by four phases. First comes the eradication of the heart, or *astonishment;* second, the *destruction of ego;* third, the achievement of *flawless concentration,* and fourth, *perfect surrender*—of even the sense of surrender. All of these phases, however, interlock with one another and do not occur in a linear fashion.

During the first phase of this journey, which we have called astonishment, the great paradox is that although the lover has achieved to a great degree a unity in understanding, he or she, in a strange turn of events, forgets even himself or herself. If he or she is asked, as Attar says, "Are you or are you not? Have you or have you not the feeling of existence? Are you in the middle or on the border? Are you mortal or immortal? He will reply with certainty, 'I am in love but with whom I do not know. My heart is at the same time both full and empty.'"[1] In this state the lover seems to lose all sense of control over his or her state and even the sense of existence is lost to him.

Why does the lover loses the sense of his or her own reality and know nothing of his or her own condition? The reason is that the faculty of perception can no longer perceive itself anymore. We "know" ourselves by the borrowed luminosity of our own minds. The mind, when it is perfectly clear, reflects the perfectly luminous radiant Atman, or higher self. When we remove this mirror, this knowing faculty, what is left is self-luminous love. It is unable to see itself through the witness of itself, but only through the Beloved. In Sufi terminology this is referred to as "losing one's heart," "eradication," or "astonishment."

"Losing the heart" of course refers not to the physical heart, but to the spiritual sense of one's entire reality. There is a beautiful Persian poem that points to this state of utter bafflement:

> *Why do you make a search for my heart,*
> *for I do not know where it is.*
> *Tell me yourself what is a heart.*
> *I do not find its trace anywhere.*[2]

Kabir made it known just how difficult it is to go beyond our self-conscious ego:

> *So what if you dropped illusion?*
> *You didn't drop your pride.*
> *Pride has fooled the best sages,*
> *Pride devours all.*[3]

This state of egoless love, in which not even the tiniest particle of pride is permitted, is a profoundly rare state. In fact, it is a state that cannot be achieved by any act of will or individual effort, but only through the will of the Beloved. As Meher Baba says:

> *Divine love arises after the disappearance*
> *of the individual mind*
> *and free from the trammels of individual nature.*[4]

Indeed, only a few hearts are fashioned for this extremity of love. Only a few hearts are ready to receive so complete a gift of love. Love, as one poet has suggested, is "that music which cannot be played on every instrument." The Indian poet Ghalib expressed this idea when he said that "love is not controllable. It is a fire which neither can be kindled nor extinguished at will."[5] To go beyond the ego, beyond the sense of "I," as Ramana Maharshi would say, is to achieve liberation.

Flawless Concentration

In order to achieve this state, however, the lover is required to perfect the art of concentration. Flawless and complete concentration, as Sant Kirpal Singh has noted, is only "another aspect of complete and total self-surrender. Whenever the 'self' enters the picture and the question of 'I'-ness arises, the single-pointedness of concentration is dissipated and inner advancement is made impossible."[6] Wherever there is perfect concentration 'I'-ness cannot arise. The 'I' of individuality asserts itself at this point and makes inner advancement impossible.

As the lover passes through this baffling state, he or she may experience both ecstasy and grief, patience and impatience, yet understand not to whom they belong. In this most wonderful phase, love has penetrated into the innermost depths of the lover, and because of this, his or her external side cannot comprehend the mystery hidden in the innermost center of his or her heart.

As love penetrates into the essence of the Beloved, it obliterates the self-conscious ego, which gives rise to any cognitive understanding of reality. As it penetrates still deeper, the very heart of the lover is consumed by love. In this condition, the lover weeps in great grief, but strangely has no sense of whom he or she is weeping for. His condition is like that of a man who has fallen asleep and in a dream meets a woman who is without equal. They spend an entire day together. Upon awakening, he is unaware of where he has been or whom he has seen. He does not know whether it was a dream or a reality. Neither does he know why he is in tears.

In this story the lover who has fallen asleep is the one who has met his or her Beloved within, but upon returning, having lost his or her self-conscious memory, can no longer remember what has happened. The lover is left in utter bafflement. The experience, however, is so profound that he or she cannot forget it either, for his or her heart has been torn asunder. In this state, Attar said there was enough sorrow for "a hundred worlds."[7]

Perfect Surrender

During this perplexing state of affairs, the lover yields up the pearl of his or her heart and surrenders everything to the Beloved. The phase of *surrender* has been mentioned in almost all scriptures, and yet there are few who really comprehend the depth of its significance.

The surrender of the mind is one of the most difficult tasks; indeed it is impossible without the grace of the Beloved. In the first place, one cannot surrender what one has no control over any more than one can give something that is not one's own. So perfect concentration precedes surrender.

The paradox of this condition is that perfect concentration produces perfect witnessing and thus the lover no longer sees through the eyes of knowledge but through "borrowed eyes" of love. If we have assumed that love has penetrated to the innermost center of the lover, there is beingness without knowledge of it. The lover cannot perceive the Beloved except with the eyes of love. His or her "experience" of the Beloved is not through knowledge but through the absenting of himself or herself.

This state is like that of the man who was in love with a woman who lived across a mighty river. Every night he would jump into the river and swim to her. One night he exclaimed, when he saw a mole on her face, "Where did this mole come from?" She answered, "I have had this mole from birth. But for your own sake, do not go into the water tonight." He did not listen, went into the river, and died of cold.

This simple parable alludes to the fact that the love of the lover is a veil upon the Beloved, and the greater his or her love the less he or she sees of the Beloved. This, in truth, is what is meant by self-surrender in its ultimate ontological sense.

Kabir tells us also that once having surrendered everything—body, wealth, possessions, and intellect—we have to surrender the very "thought of surrender" or the Seed Mind.

Sant Kirpal Singh summarizes the qualities that make up the perfect state of surrender when he talks of:

Complete obedience born out of love,
with no conditions, with no hope of any return,
expecting absolutely nothing in return,
with no choice left.[8]

In this state there is no question of choice, for there is no reality other than that of the Beloved. Choice arises only when there is still some aspect of the interior heart that does not participate in love, that has not been fully subdued. Only a part of the heart that does not dwell fully in the Beloved can believe it has the choice of whether or not to be in the Beloved. Choice presupposes a sense of duality. In the exalted state of perfect self-surrender, even the sense of a separate existence has been consumed, and choice has no place.

Love, in these ultimate states, admits no cognitive understanding. Comprehension and apprehension both are experiences viewed through the limitations of the faculties of sight, hearing, smell, taste, and touch. Ultimate spiritual realities, on the other hand, can never be *known* by anyone; they can only be *become*. In this sense we affirm what Saint Paul said when he remarked that "nobody has ever seen God"—that is, God without form (John 1: 18).

In Jewish mystical literature, the notion of self-surrender is a very old one and finds expression in many Kabbalistic texts. For the Zadik (spiritual mentor) everything must be surrendered in the name of YHWH. In this primal act of self-surrender the mystic tells us that "he who utterly surrenders his soul to the name of YHWH will dwell and establish its throne and glory."[9]

For the Jewish mystic, as with all other lovers, the act of "giving up the self" is central to the consummation of the lover-Beloved relationship. The point here is that no matter what religious tradition we profess, the actual experience of union transcends the confines of both Eastern and Western dogmas. Mysticism, in fact, transcends all outer or esoteric aspects of religion, for religion conveys concepts about unity and not unity itself. C. G. Jung once observed that religions are in fact a defense against the religious experience. Devotees frequently, instead of trying to actually experience these transcendent states, choose to conceptualize them, and by so doing remove themselves one more step from the actual religious experience. Understanding is not being.

For the true lover who has awakened to the light of love, there is no seeing and no existence apart from the Beloved. In fact, there is nothing but the Beloved.

In proceeding through this valley, the lover passes beyond the confines of time. Here the lover is not tied down by the stations of contraction (sorrow) or expansion (ecstasy). Neither is he or she concerned with separation or union, delight or sorrow, or any changing state.

The lover, who was previously under the control of time, and hence subject to change, is now the commander of time and in the decision-making position. Having passed from all contrary states, the lover rests in the changeless state of God beyond time. In this realm nothing can pierce the darkness of the black light save the all-luminous Beloved. And in order to pass through this realm the Beloved absorbs the lover completely. This the Sufis indicate this by the phrase "becoming a hair in the Beloved's tresses."[10]

Now having effaced the condition of change and time, having completely shattered the idols of falsity, greed, and illusion (death, desire, and ego), transcended the three bodies (physical, astral, and causal), the mystery of the origins of creation *(parusha* and *prakiti)*, the void of nothingness *(maha sunn* of the Saints, *nirodh* of the Buddhists, and *lahoot* stage of the Sufis) and the state of God beyond God or Pav Brahm, he or she enters the final journey.

Following page:
Standing Buddha
Sarnatti Musee, Paris

In this early pre-Christian sculpture of the Buddha, he stands in the "pose of perfection" with one hand (broken off) facing up to receive divine energy and the other facing down, emanating the divine flow. Buddha, the universal human, the supreme symbol of consciousness, is depicted as a conscious co-worker in the divine plan.

CHAPTER 11

Enslavement

When love reaches its highest goal
Love turns entirely into enmity.

—Rumi

Some Sufis have called this station "the valley of destruction and deprivation"; others have referred to it as enslavement and annihilation. Most mystics and Masters have written very sparingly on the subject; in fact, if one were to survey the entire stock of religious literature, one probably would find hardly a volume dealing directly with it.

And yet it is precisely here that the most important stage of the journey is completed. Farid Attar has said that "the essence of this valley is forgetfulness, dumbness, deafness, and distraction."[1] The Master Chiragh-i-Delhi describes this phase as concealment, leading to dread of losing the Beloved's love, which leads to bewilderment, supplication, distraction, and finally destruction. Although this exalted state is quite beyond the conception of the mind, and hence even descriptions of these states must be grossly inadequate, the saints and mystics have spoken metaphorically of these profound changes and transformations. Here, as Attar has said, the world becomes but a play of shadows in the immensity of "a single ray of the celestial sun."[2]

It has also been likened to an immense ocean which, when it begins to heave, patterns on its surface lose their form. This form and pattern is no other than the present world and the world to come. When in this state, we are reduced to ashes.

A story describes how someone once saw Majnun making an image of Leila and himself in the soil. Then Majnun effaced the image of Leila. The passerby remarked, "What sort of love is it which makes the lover efface the sketch of the Beloved?"

Majnun said in reply, "If you do not find Leila in me, then make another sketch of her." A poet wrote of this story:

> *When someone carves the lover's image*
> *The Beloved emerges out of it.*[3]

Distraction

Ahmad Ghazzali has given us a profound insight into the psychology of the transformative search for the Beloved. In this final state, *distraction*, the sign of "love's perfection is that the Beloved becomes the lover's affliction, so that he or she cannot possibly have the strength to bear her and cannot carry her weight, and he stands waiting by the door of annihilation."[4] In this state, the lover finds rest neither in the presence of the Beloved nor away from Her. In this paradox of existence, the knot of unity is finally tied. This "continuity of affliction" in the end produces "the continuity of seeing." The poet speaks of this enigma when he says,

> *No one is like me so miserable,*
> *For I am in grief both when I see you*
> *And when I see you not.*[5]

Love, then, in its near perfect state, is when the form of the Beloved becomes the image of the lover's spirit. When love reaches its perfect state, it subsists through and of itself, without anything outside it, including the Beloved. Until love is self-subsisting within itself, there is still not perfect love.

There are three very unique phases to the binding of love-consciousness. The first phase, as has already been intimated, is when the lover reaches that state of purity of which Darshan Singh writes:

I have reached that state of bliss,
that state of ecstasy, that state of perfect peace,
that state of self-oblivion
where there is only Sawan [His Beloved]
there is no trace of me.[6]

In this state the mind of the lover is so pure that it functions as the *mirror of the Beloved.* A Muslim divine descibes this state as follows:

The place inside is so filled with my Beloved
That there is no room for me.
In you am I, look in my eyes and see the Oneness.
If you do not see, am I to be blamed?[7]

In the middle phase, *knowledge,* is also added to the experience of union. Yet this knowledge is not of an objectifiable reality, but of a noetic, existential one. Here, the lover not only contemplates the form of the Beloved, but is given knowledge that he or she is aware of that union. Although from an ordinary point of view it would appear that such a state would imply the positionality of subject and object; in fact both subject and object are identified with one another.

This phase has been described by the poets as "drinking wine and being told they are becoming drunk." In this state the lover sees not only the Beloved's form but his or her own form within the form of the Beloved. Speaking of this experience Kabir said, "One entered all, All entered that. The Knowledge beyond knowledge is my knowledge."

Obliteration

The last phase of the state of union is in fact the only real union, for here the ultimate ontological reality is reached, which is the *obliteration* of both subject and object. In this state there is no sign of either the Beloved or the lover, for both, as we have explained earlier, are branches of the tree of love itself. At this stage, there is only undifferentiated awareness, not of anything; but in an absolute sense of itself being nothing else but love.

The concept of annihilation or obliteration is a difficult one for Western readers. Such negative imagery often brings to mind thoughts of total extinction or lifelessness. Terms like "annihilation" may, to our ears, set up a sense of dualism that does not reflect the essential oneness of love.

For the lover, the experience of divine love is always one of expansiveness and inclusivity, even in its initial stages. True love can never be confined within any boundaries and defies the dualism of "I" and "other." Annihilation in this phase indicates the obliteration of a sense of separate existence, conditioned by the illusory experience of mind and matter. The cosmic embrace with divine love obliterates every aspect of limitation and reveals the Self as the primordial reality. The Qur'an affirms this divine condition: "He who knows himself knows his Lord."

Sant Darshan gives us a wonderful depiction of this state:

What does it matter if I am called a man?
In reality I am the very soul of love.
The entire earth is my home,
and the universe my country.[8]

Mystic poets like Rumi, Sant Darshan, Attar, Hildegard of Bingen, Meister Eckhart, Kabir, and many others have testified to the wonderful, incomprehensible essence of this Being whose presence consumes a hundred thousand worlds in a moment. Despite the outer shell of differences in language, culture and religion, the experience of unity defies cultural and religious singularities. Meister Eckhart says,

In this breaking-through I find that God and I
are both the same.
Then I am what I was, I neither wax nor wane,
for I am the motionless cause that is moving all things.[9]

The obliteration of differentiation is in essence the nature of realization. Yoga Darshana describes it thus: "When alone the object of contemplation remains and one's form is annihilated, this is known as identification."[10] This identification is none other than "unification, which is the separation of the eternal from that which was originated in time." The Buddha insisted upon a non-dual reality as the primary characteristic of realization. The Buddhist does not speak of "love" but of "emptiness." This no-thingness is itself pure awareness. Of what, one may ask? It is awareness of itself. Sengtsan says, "In the World of Reality there is no self, there is no other than Self." All beings are "the Buddha nature."[11]

Union

In the final analysis there is no analysis possible. There are no questions and no answers; *that which is, is.* Since these states are not rational, the mystic writers merely point to reassuring signs along the road for those who have entered upon the Great Journey. Lao Tzu recognized this dilemma when he says in the Tao Te Ching:

The Way that can be told
Is not the constant way;
The name that can be named,
Is not the constant name.[12]

Kabir, finding it impossible to describe, said:

If I say it's one, it isn't so
If I say it's two, it's slander
Kabir has thought about it.
As it is,
So it is.[13]

It is this truth that all realization is meant to attain. The final attainment in fact is no attainment at all; it is merely the removal of illusion. The Supreme Godhead, the essence of Love, is a state beyond conceptualization. Sant Kirpal Singh explains that even the *full effulgence of light* referred to as *sach khand* in the Sikh scriptures, as *muqum-i-Haq* by the Sufis, and as *the New Jerusalem* in the Christian scriptures, is not the final realization. As he notes, "in the higher planes of *Sat naam* [literally "place of truth"], the soul goes on being absorbed until it comes into the wordless state, where there is no light or sound."

Of this placeless place or stateless state, very little can be said. Guru Nanak, the first guru of the Sikhs, gives us a poetic summary of the residence of the Supreme Being when he says in the prologue to the Sikh scriptures:

There is One Reality, the Unmanifest-manifest.
Ever-Existent, He is Naam [conscious spirit].
The creator pervading all;
Without fear, without enmity;
The Timeless; the Unborn; and the Self-existent;
Complete within Itself.[14]

Other Masters, mystics, and saints have in their own way sought to explain this "Mysterium Magnum." Meister Eckhart used much the same words to describe the same thing:

What is the last end?
It is the mystery of the darkness of the eternal Godhead
which is unknown and never has been known.
Therein, God abides to Himself unknown.[15]

Using Sufi terminology, the Sufi Master Jili replies:

The Divine Obscurity is the primordial place,
Where the suns of beauty set.
It is the Self of God Himself.[16]

Or again, should we have any doubt, these mystics' words are reinforced by another great Christian mystic, Jacob Boehme, "God has made all things out of nothing, and that same nothing is Himself."

Plato, too, glimpsed this reality: "There abides the very being with which true knowledge is concerned: the colorless, formless, intangible essence...knowledge absolute is existence absolute."[17]

And finally in the *Sefer Yetsirah*, with classical rabinical humor and simplicity, it is written:

Before the One, what is there to count?[18]

What, then, is the consummation of the lover-Beloved relationship? Who is the lover? The lover is pure essence. What is love? It is the subsistence of the essence of things. The Sufi saint Jami, explains the ontological beginning of this relationship in one of his poems, says:

Non-existence fell in love with Existence.
The Non-existent through this Love became existent.
Then non-existence was graced with
the Light of Existence,
its aspiration moved to its source.
The attraction of love holds together
the shadow and the sun.[19]

What then is the lover, but the Beloved in disguise? What then is the Beloved but the essence of love? What, we might ask, could arise out of truth, save truth? Indeed, what can possibly rise out of love, save love?

Love is the hidden secret about which it is said in the Quran, "I was a hidden treasure and desired to be known." Jami and many others see love as the primal attribute of the Divine Essence. In truth God is making love unto Himself, by Himself, and to Himself endlessly. When in pre-temporality, before the appearance of creation, love was both essence and attribute, and yet causeless and without beginning.

In order, as some Sufis have said, for God to know and experience His own essence, otherness was required. This otherness was itself latent in the very nature of love. It was not need, because perfect love is without need, complete in itself. In its expression as otherness, as lover and Beloved, what was latent in love became manifest. One poet, whose name is unknown (possibly Hazrat Inayat Khan), has tried to capture this paradox:

He has rendered the world into a mirror wherein
He shows Himself unto Himself.
All that is seen or unseen
is but a reflection of His Beauty.
When that Beauty desired to come
in the form of Glory,
It put on the visage of this world of time and space.
Whose is any name? Whose is any identity?

Is there anything here and there other than Him?
He alone is there
under every name and under every identity.[20]

God beholds His own beauty and loves it, and this we may call love in post-temporality. Love, then, in quite a paradoxical way, is not characterized by either union or separation. The experience of union is the attribute of the Beloved, while the experience of separation is the attribute of the lover.

Primordial Beginning

We have arrived, then, at the primordial beginning, because in love the end must become the beginning, for there is neither beginning nor end. As Sant Darshan has remarked, "Love has only a beginning, it has no end."[21] The journey through time from pre-temporality to post- temporality is a journey through the illusion of duality. It is a movement through "existence" to "beingness," from form to formlessness. The journey of love is implied not only in every creature but in every atom of creation. For the source of otherness, whether an atom or a sun, lies in pre-temporality and henceforth. Rumi expressed this wonderfully:

When was I ever less by dying...
Yet once more I shall die as man, to soar,
With angels blessed; but even from angelhood
I must pass on; all except God doth perish.

When I have sacrificed my angel-soul,
I shall become what no mind ever conceived.
Oh let me not exist; for nonexistence
Proclaims in organ tones, "To Him we shall return."[22]

After arriving at their final destination, the lovers, according to the Sufi saint, Ibn Arabi, are "affirmed, then made present, then made to remain, then gathered together, then assigned." One who remains at the destination, according to Ibn Arabi, is called *waqif* or "one who stops." These souls do not return with a mission from God but remain absorbed in that state that is in fact neither a place nor a state.

Among those who return, Sant Kirpal Singh has distinguished two types of gurus. They are the *Swateh Sant* gurus, who come into the world as perfected beings, and *Sants* who complete the course during their current lifetime. The only difference is that one comes with authority, while the other "acquires authority while here."[23] Both, however, come with a mission and work for the salvation of mankind by authority of the Supreme Being.

Such perfected beings remain thirsty forever. The journey *to* God is limited since it "means crossing the ocean of existence. But the journey *in* God...is infinite,"[24] because His attributes are endless and without limit. So satiation is unimaginable to the perfect lover of God. And the journey we speak of is in God, through God, and by God.

Following page:
Standing Shiva
National Museum, Madras

This early bronze figure of Shiva depicts the creative and destructive aspects of the universe, synthesized in the perfect lover. Neither life nor death have any power over the perfect lover, and Shiva is the symbol of this unification of being.

Death:
The Final Beginning

What though I die hourly,
I have each time found a better life.

—Angelus Silesius

With the above words, Angelus Silesius sums up the life of the mystic, not only during this life, but at the moment of final departure from this world as well.

At every moment the mystic lover is "dying to his or her small selves so that the larger self may emerge." But the paradox of the lover's path is precisely this, that at every moment of death there is a corresponding moment of birth and the two are quite interdependent. It is only in the final death that the soul, as the Sufis say, "passes away into God," where there is no further transformation. At that moment there is only God, the self-existent, eternal and immutable mystery of pure Being.

For the lover, all births and all deaths are part of a progression toward pure Being. Though powerful experiences on the human level, they are merely sign posts, part of the changing panorama of illusion. Human death is simply a cousin to the inevitable death in God. The Qur'an sums up the lover's understanding with these words:

All things perish save His countenance.

In this context, the process of *initiation* is seen as the first of many spiritual deaths of the lover, one in which the state of illusion is first challenged by the force of love. Love is a standing challenge to duality; it beckons us on to ever more permanent states of being. While the lover is living in this world, the lover's life represents the uniting creative action of love on all levels. Saint Paul said:

For me to live is Christ,
and to die is gain.

Dying Daily

Death, for the mystic, is a way of life, in which all things are consumed in the great fire of love. The real lover is one who already has died to his or her physical body, and traverses freely into other worlds unfettered by earthly encumbrances. He or she further dies to his or her astral body and finally to his or her causal body, each of which represents a further transition from illusion to reality, from death to immortality. Throughout mystic literature and poetry, the lover is portrayed as *one who has already died*. The prophet Mohammed said, "Die before you Die." Rumi encapsulated this truth with the words:

One Reason to gain eternal life
tread everlastingly the way of death.[1]

The practice of spiritual dying is as old as existence itself. Entering the spiritual path is a dying to our small selves. Every moment of our lives is asking that we die and die again. For in each death the ego, which for the lover is the symbol of separation, is put to another death. Death, as Philalethes, the seventeenth-century English Hermetic philosopher said, "must precede perfect union."[2] It could virtually be said that every page of Meister Eckart's works proclaims death. Ramana Maharshi has said, as have all the non-dualists, that "one cannot see God and yet retain individuality."[3]

The lover is one who has become an expert at annihilation, for it is only in annihilation "that we discover the beautiful face of the bride."[4] The divine lover, as we have seen in the preceding chapters, learns this art of dying, while living so that there is absolutely nothing, not even his or her very self, to which he or she has not died. Death is both sign and symbol of the destruction of "I" consciousness. Sri Sankaracharya once said, "He is the knower of the Self to whom the ideas of 'me' and 'mine' have become quite meaningless."[5]

The Death of Saints

Those who have "broken this idol of clay," as Rumi put it, find the face of the Beloved gloriously before them. At the moment the soul cleaves from the body in physical death, it is reunited with the Beloved. Death is the vehicle for the lover's final initiation. Sant Kirpal Singh states the position of saints who have already "passed away in God":

The lovers know where and how to die,
They accept and relish death as a gift from the Beloved.
With inner eye opened, they see the glory of God,
When others are forced blindfolded
into the blind alley.[6]

Angelus Silesius wrote:

I say since death alone delivers me,
It is of all things the best of things.[7]

The Death of Distinction

The final death is the *death of the distinction between life and death*. Having subdued within himself or herself the distinction between life and death, what is left for the lover is always a beginninng. For the love that dwells in unity, death is not opposed to love, but the mirror in which it is reflected. The lover who faces his or her end faces no end at all. He or she faces only the supreme Friend, and a new beginning.

Following page:
Christ Enthroned upon a Cloud
Metropolitan Museum of Art, New York

In this sixteenth-century enamel by Leonard Limousin, Christ is depicted as the *Logos*, the divine center of the universe, with radiance emanating from his form. Here the Divine Beloved receives the feminine symbol of receptivity in the form of his mother, Mary, and blesses his father, Joseph.

Notes

Introduction

1. Meher Baba, *Meher Baba on Love* (Poona: Meher Baba Publishing, 1966), p. 85.

2. Robert Johnson, *We: Understanding the Psychology of Romantic Love* (New York, Harper & Row, 1983), pp. 146–150.

3. Denis de Rougemont, *Love in the Western World*, trans. Montgomery Belgion (New York: Pantheon Books, 1956), pp. 51–52.

4. Johnson, pp. 147–150.

5. *Ibid.*, pp. 146–156.

6. Quoted in Sant Darshan Singh, *Love at Every Step* (Bowling Green, Va.: Sawan Kirpal Publications, 1989), p. 95.

7. Mir Valiudin, *Love of God* (Farnham, England: Sufi Publishing, 1972), p. 128.

8. Ibin-Farid, *Khamriyya* (Paris: Editions Vega, 1931), verse 37.

9. All biblical references are to the King James Version and the Douay Edition are cited hereafter in the text.

10. Plato, "Phaedrus," *Dialogues of Plato* , trans. Benjamin Jowett, 4th ed., (Oxford: Claredon Press, 1953).

11. Rumi, *Mathnawi*, trans. Reynold A. Nicholson (London: Luzac, 1936), Vol. 2, p. 2328.

12. John Smith, *Select Discourses 1618–1652* (London: Cambridge University Press, 1821), p. 300.

13. Sant Darshan Singh, *Secret of Secrets* (Bowling Green, Va.: Sawan Kirpal Publications, 1982).

14. Margaret Smith, *Mystics of Islam* (London: Luzac, 1950), p. 91.

Chapter One

1. René Guenon, *Apercus L'Initiation* (Paris: Editions Traditionelles, 1964), p. 273.

2. Meister Eckhart, *Meister Eckhart*, trans. Franz Pfeiffer (London: John Murray Press, 1961), Vol. I, p. 275.

3. Guenon, p. 219.

4. *Ha Zohar Book of Splendour*, trans. Daniel Chanan Matt (New York: Paulist Press, 1983).

5. Sant Kirpal Singh, *Sat Sandesh* (Tilton, N.H.: Sant Bani Press, 1971), p. 2.

6. Mir Muhammad Hayat, *Misbah-ul-Hayut* (Bombay: Fat-hul-Furim Press, 1906), p. 1.

7. Shrivatsa Goswami, *The Divine Consort*, ed. John Stratton Hawley and Donna Marie Wolf (Boston: Beacon Press, 1987), p. 79.

8. Kirpal Singh, *Sat Sandesh* (Tilton, N.H.: Sant Bani Press, August 1972), p. 1.

9. Margaret Smith, *Mystics of Islam*, p. 91.

10. Coomaraswamy, *Hinduism and Buddhism* (New York: Philosophical Librarian Publishers, 1943), Vol. 1, p. 294.

11. Emile Dermenghen, *Vies des Santo Musulmans* (Algiers: Baconnier, n.d.), pp. 113-114.

12. Mir Valiudin, *Love of God* (Farnham, England: Sufi Publishing, 1972), p. 32.

13. Sant Darshan Singh, *Secret of Secrets* (Bowling Green, Va.: Sawan Kirpal Publications, 1982).

14. Al Yafi i, *Rawdh al Rayahin*, quoted in Emile Dermenghem, *Vies des Santo Musulmans* (Algiers: Baconnier, n.d.), p. 348.

15. Quoted by Mir Valiudin, *Love of God* (Farnham, England: Sufi Publishing, 1972), pp. 35–45.

16. Darshan Singh, *Secret of Secrets* (Bowling Green, Va.: Kirpal Publications, 1982), p. 249.

17. Rumi, *Mathnawi*, trans. Reynold A. Nicholson, (London: Luzac, 1936), Vol. 1, p. 1435.

Chapter Two

1. Whitnall N. Perry, *The Treasury of Traditional Wisdom* (New York: Simon & Schuster, 1962), p. 23.

2. Sant Kirpal Singh, *Godman* (Delhi: Ruhani Sat Sang, 1967).

3. Swami Ramdas, *World Is God* (Kanhangad, India: Ananda Ashram, 1955), p. 255.

4. Quoted in Emile Dermenghem, *Vies des Santo Musulmans*, (Algiers: Baconnier, n.d.), p. 202.

5. Sant Kirpal Singh, *Night Is a Jungle* (Tilton, N.H.: Sant Bani Press, 1973), p. 251.

6. Jalaluddin Rumi, *Mathnawi* (London: Luzac 1926-1934), Vol. 3, p. 2548.

7. Sant Kirpal Singh, *Sat Sandesh* (periodical), November 1975, p. 4.

8. W. D. Begg, *Hazrat Khwaja Moinuddin Chisti* (Tucson, Ariz.: Chisti Sufi Mission of America, 1977), p. 148.

9. Swami Sivananda, *Japa Yoga* (Rishiskesh, India: Yoga Vedanta Forest University, 1952), pp. 107–109.

10. Thomas Norton, *Ordinall of Alchemy* (1652; facsimile reprint, London: Edward Arnold, 1928), p. 14.

11. Chang Po-Tuan, Essay on "The Understanding of Truth," trans. Tenny L. Davis and Chao Yun Tsung in *Proceedings of American Academy of Arts and Science*, Vol. 73, No. 5, July 1939, p. 111.

12. Sawan Singh, *A Pictorial Biography, Glimpses of the Great Master* (Hong Kong: Radha Swami Satsang Beas, 1986), p. 54.

13. Ramana Maharshi, *Talks with Sri Ramana Maharshi*, 3 vol., ed., T. N. Venkataraman (South India: Tiruvannamalai, 1955), pp. 499–500.

14. Ahmad Ghazzali, *Sawanih*, trans. Nasorollah Pourjavady, quoted in *Bayazid al Bistami* (London: Routledge and Kegan Paul and Iran University Press, 1986), p. 23.

15. Kabir, quoted in Sant Kirpal Singh, *Sat Sandesh*, Nov. 10, 1973, p. 2.

16. Mir Valiudin, *Love of God* (Farnham, England: Sufi Publishing, 1972), p. 203.

17. Alphonsus Liguori, *Conformity to the Will of God* (Clyde, Mo.: Benedictine Convent of Perpetual Adoration, 1935) pp. 42–43.

Chapter Three

1. Mir Valiudin, *Love of God* (Farnham, England: Sufi Publishing, 1972), p. 12.

2. Attar, *The Conference of the Birds*, trans. C. S. Nott (New York: Samuel Weiser, 1969), p. 102.

3. Sant Kirpal Singh, *Sat Sandesh* (Bowling Green, Va.: Sawan Kirpal Publications, February 2).

4. Bhai Nanlal Goya, quoted in *Sat Sandesh* (Bowling Green, Va.: Sawan Kirpal Publications, June 1976), p. 30.

5. Kabir, quoted in *Sat Sandesh* (Bowling Green, Va.: Sawan Kirpal Publications, June 1976), pp. 30-31.

6. Mir Valiudin, *Love of God* (Farnham, England: Sufi Publishing, 1972), p. 15.

7. Stephen Clissold, quoted in *The Wisdom of the Spanish Mystics* (New York: New Directions, 1977), pp. 40–41.

8. Li Liweng, *My Country and My People* (London: Heinemann, 1951), p. 235.

9. Ali Hujiwir, *Khasf al Mahjub*, trans. R. A. Nicholson (London: Luzac, 1911), p. 299.

10. Sant Darshan Singh, *A Tear and a Star* (Bowling Green, Va.: Sawan Kirpal Publishing , 1986), p. 10.

11. Tulsi Das, *Kavitovali* (London: George Allen & Unwin, 1964), p. 161.

12. Frithjup Schuon, *Stations of Wisdom* (London: John Murray, 1961), p. 145.

Chapter Four

1. Mir Valiudin, *Love of God* (Farnham, England: Sufi Publishing, 1972), p. 168.

2. *Ibid.*, p. 24.

3. Al Ghazzali, *Sawanih* (London: KPI, 1986), p. 44.

4. Saint John of Ruysbroeck, *The Advancement of the Spiritual Marriage II*, trans. C. A. Wyncshen, ed. Evelyn Underhill (London: John M. Watkins, 1951), p. 131.

5. Yoga Vasishtha, *The World within the Mind*, trans. Hari Prasad Shastri (London: Shanti Sada, 1937), p. 132.

6. Sant Kirpal Singh, *Sat Sandesh* (Tilton, N.H.: Sant Bani Press, January 1971), p. 12.

7. *Ibid.*, p. 12.

8. Kabir, *The Bijak*, trans. Linda Hess and Shukdev Singh (San Francisco: North Point Press, 1983), p. 82.

9. Sant Darshan Singh, *Secret of Secrets* (Bowling Green, Va.: Kirpal Publications, 1982), pp. 252–253.

10. Mir Valiudin, *Love of God* (Farnham, England: Sufi Publishing, 1972), Chapter One, Chapter Two.

11. Al Ghazzali, *Ihyu Ulûm al–Dîn, or the Revivification of Religion, IV* (Delhi: Bharitiya Vidya Bhavan, 1959), pp. 275–278.

Chapter Five

1. Attar, *The Conference of the Birds* (New York: Samuel Weiser, 1954), p. 102.

2. Pearle Epstein, *Kabbalah: The Way of the Jewish Mystic* (New York: Doubleday), pp. 126–127.

3. Quoted in Kirpal Singh, *Sat Sandesh*, April 1974, p. 5.

4. Ahmad Ghazzali, *The Sawainih, or Inspiration from the World of Pure Spirits*, trans. Nasrollah Pourjavady (London: KPI and Iran University Press, 1986), p. 46.

5. Kabir, *The Bijak*, trans. Linda Hess and Shukdev Singh (San Francisco: North Point Press, 1983), p. 35.

6. Quoted in Ken Wilber, *No Boundary* (Los Angeles: Center Publishing House, 1979), p. 63.

7. Bahari Bankey, *Mystic Saints and Masters* (Delhi: Bharitiya Vidya Bhavan, 1971), p. 61.

8. Quoted in Coomaraswamy: *Hinduism and Buddhism* (New York: Philosophical Library, 1948), pp. 20–21.

Chapter Six

1. Farrid uddin Attar, *Memorial of the Saints*, trans. Pavet de Courteille (London: Royal Asiatic Society, 1917).

2. Huzur Baba Sawan Singh Ji, the esteemed twentieth–century saint of Beas known as the Master of Surat Shabd Yoga.

3. Saint John of the Cross, *Dark Night of the Soul*, trans. Kieran Kauanaught and Otilo Rodriguez, Book 2, Chapter Five, Chapter Nine.

4. Attar, *The Conference of the Birds* (New York: Samuel Weiser, 1954), p. 64.

5. Sant Darshan Singh, *Secret of Secrets*, (Bowling Green, Va.: Sawan Kirpal Publications, 1982), p. 250.

6. *Ibid.*, p. 256.

7. *Ibid.*, p. 251.

8. Mir Valiudin, *Love of God* (Farnham, England: Sufi Publishing, 1972), p. 22.

Chapter Seven

1. Quoted by Kirpal Singh, *Sat Sandesh* (Tilton, N.H.: Sant Bani Press, Oct. 1976), pp. 10–11.

2. Ahmad Ghazzali, *The Sawanih* (London: KPI, 1985), p. 23.

3. *Ibid.*, p. 24.

4. Thomas a Kempis, *The Imitation of Christ* (New York: Thomas Y. Crowell, n.d.), Vol. 7, p. III.

5. *Ramana Maharshi, Talks with Sri Ramana Maharshi, 3 vols.*, (Tiruvannamalai, South India: T. N. Venkatraman, n. d.), p. 158.

6. Shabistari, *Mystic Rose Garden*, trans. F. Lederer (Lahore: Ashraf Publications), p. 77.

7. Ananda Moyi Ma, *Aux Sources de la Joie*, trans. Jean Herbert (Calcutta: Ophyris, 1943), p. 28.

8. Rumi (attrib.), *Divan Shamsi Tabriz XXXXI*, in *Selected Poems of the Divani Shamsi Tabriz*, trans. R. A. Nicholson (Cambridge, Mass.: University Press, 1952).

9. Satprem, *Sri Aurobindo or the Adventure of Consciousness*, trans. Themi (Pondicherry, India: All India Press, 1970), p. 158.

Chapter Eight

1. Attar, *The Conference of the Birds* (New York: Samuel Weiser Publications, 1954), p. 116.

2. Quoted by Mir Valiudin, *Love of God* (New York: Sufi Publishing, 1972), p. 20.

3. Leon Stein, "Hasidic Music," *The Chicog Jewish Forum*, Vol. II, No. 1 (Fall 1943), p. 16.

4. Chandoga Unpanishad, from the Thirteen Principal Upanishads, trans. Robert Hume (Oxford: Oxford University Press, 1934), VI, XI 3.

5. Lankavatara Sutra (Mayahana Buddhist scripture), VII.

6. *Dhamapada*, trans. Max Muller (Oxford, England: 1898), pp. 153–154.

7. Mother Teresa, quoted in Jean Houston, *In Search for the Beloved* (New York: Tarcher Press, 1988), p. 134.

8. Sengtsan, quoted by Angelus Silesius in Frederick Frank, *The Book of Angelus Silesius* (New York: Knopf, 1976), p. 49.

9. Attar, *The Conference of the Birds* (New York: Samuel Weiser, 1954), p. 117.

10. *Gospel of Sri Rama Krishna*, trans. Swami Nikhilanada (New York: Rama Krishna Vedanta Center, 1942), p. 223.

Chapter Nine

1. *Divan of Hafiz*, trans. Mehdi K. Nakosteen (Boulder, Colo.: University of Colorado Press, 1973), p. 341.

2. Bijak Kabir, trans. Linda Hess (New York: Harper & Row, 1983), p. 103.

3. Matilda of Magdeburg, *The Revelations of Matilda of Magdeburg*, trans. Lucy Menzies (London: Longmans, Green, 1953), p. 22.

4. Mir Valiudin, *Love of God* (Farnham, England: Sufi Pub., 1972), p. 12.

5. *Ibid.*, p. 13.

6. Saint Isaac of Syria, *Writings from the Philokalia on Prayer of the Heart*, trans. E. Kadloubovsky and G.E.H. Palmer (London: Faber and Faber, 1951), p. 258.

7. Al Ghazzali, *The Revivification of Religion,* trans. Margaret Smith (London: Luzac, 1950), p. 72.

8. *Richard of Saint Victor*, trans. Clare Kirchberger (London: Faber and Faber, 1957), p. 63.

9. Omar Khayyam, *Rubaiyat*, trans. Edward Fitzgerald (London: 1859), 5th ed., verse 59.

10. Nablusi (Abdu 'l Ghani al Nablusi), quoted in Emile Dermenghem, *L'Eloge du Vin* (Paris: Editions Vega, 1931), p. 110.

11. Khwaja Hafiz, cited in Coomaraswamy, *Am I My Brother's Keeper?* (New York: John Kaym, 1947), p. 100.

12. Darshan Singh, *The Cry of the Soul* (Bowling Green. Va.: Sawan Kirpal Publications, 1977), p. 49.

13. Rama Krishna-Sri, *The Gospel According to Rama Krishna*, ed., Swami Nikhilananda (New York: Rama Krishna Vedanta Center, 1945).

14. Ahmad Ghazzali, *Sawanih* (London: KPI, 1986), p. 44.

15. Paul Oskar Kristello, *Philosophy of Marsilio Fecino* (New York: Columbia University Press, 1943), p. 228.

16. Sant Darshan Singh, *A Tear and a Star* (Bowling Green, Va.: Sawan Kirpal Publications, 1986), p. 25.

17. Ahmad Ghazzali, *Sawanih* (New York: KPI, 1986), pp. 44–45.

Chapter Ten

1. Attar, *The Conference of the Birds,* (New York: Samuel Weiser Publications, 1954), p. 119.

2. Mir Valiudin, *Love of God* (Farnham, England: Sufi Publishing House, 1972), p. 29.

3. Kabir, *Bijak*, trans. Linda Hess (New York: Harper & Row, 1983), pp. 106, 140.

4. Meher Baba, *Discourses of Meher Baba* (Tokyo: Komiyama, 1967), p. 163.

5. Ghalib, cited by Mir Valiudin, *Love of God* (Sufi Publications, England, 1972), p. 29.

6. Sant Kirpal Singh, *Night is a Jungle* (Tilton, N. H.: Sant Bani Publications, 1975), p. 272.

7. Attar, *The Conference of the Birds,* p. 123.

8. Kabir, quoted in Kirpal Singh, *Godman* (Delhi, India: Ruhani Satsang Publications, 1968), p. 119.

9. Moses de Leon, quoted in *Major Trends in Jewish Mysticism* (New York: Schocken Books, 1954), p. 223.

10. Ahmad Ghazzali, *Sawanih*, trans. N. Pourjady (London: KPI, 1986), p. 39.

Chapter Eleven

1. Attar, *The Conference of the Birds* (New York: Samuel Weiser Publications, 1954), p. 123.

2. *Ibid.*, p. 126

3. Ahmad Ghazzali, *Sawanih* (London: KPI, 1986), p.68.

4. *Ibid.*, p. 69.

5. *Ibid.*, p. 69.

6. Sant Darshan Singh, *A Tear and a Star* (Bowling Green, Va.: Sawan Kirpal Publications, 1986), p. 55.

7. Kirpal Singh, *Night Is a Jungle* (Tilton, N. H.: Sant Bani Press, 1975), p. 277.

8. Sant Darshan Singh, *A Tear and a Star*, p. 55.

9. Meister Eckhart, *Meister Eckhart*, trans. C. de B. Evans (London: John Watkins, n. d.), p. 221.

10. Yoga Darshana (comprises the Yoga Sutras of Patangali and Commentary of Vyasa), quoted in Alain Danielou, *Yoga, the Method of Re-Integration* (London: Christopher Johnson, 1949), p. 221.

11. Frederick Franck, *Book of Angelius Silesius* (New York: Knopf, 1976), p. 5.

12. *Lao Tzu*, trans. Chu Tu Kao (London: Buddhist Lodge,1937).

13. Kabir, *Bijak*, trans. Linda Hess and Shukdev Singh (San Francisco: Northpoint Press, 1983), p. 103.

14. Kirpal Singh, *The Jap ji* (Bowling Green, Va.: Sawan Kirpal Publications, 1981), p. 87.

15. Meister Eckhart, *Meister Eckhart*, trans. C. de B. Evans (London: John Watkins), p. 224.

16. Jili, *Al-Insan al-Kamil (The Universal Man)*, trans. Titus Burckhart (Lyon: P. Derain, 1921), p. 54.

17. Jacob Boehme, *Signatura Rerum: The Signature of All Things*, trans. William Law, 4 vols. (New York: 1912–1921), vol. 4, p. 9.

18. Plato, *The Dialogues of Plato*, trans. Benjamin Jowett, 4th ed. (Oxford: Clarendon Press, 1953), p. 247.

19. *Sefer Yetsirah, Book of Creation*, quoted in René Guenon, *Le Symbolisme de La Croix*, (Paris: Editions Vega, 1931), p. 45.

20. Jami Nur al Din Add-al Rahman, *Flashes of Light*, trans. H. Whinfield (London: Royal Asiatic Society, 1906-1928), p. XII.

21. Sant Darshan, *A Tear and a Star* (Bowling Green, Va.: Sawan Kirpal Publications, 1986), p. 2.

22. Rumi, *Mathnawi* (London: Luzac, 1926-1934).

23. Kirpal Singh, *Godman* (Delhi: Ruhani Sat Sang, 1967), pp. 17–18.

24. Ibn Arabi, *Journey to the Lord of Power* (New York: Inner Tradition, 1981), pp. 63-64.

Chapter Twelve

1. Work attributed to Rumi, in commemoration of his Master, Shamsi Tabriz. All quotations are taken from Selected Poems from the Divani Shamsi Tabriz, trans. R. A. Nicholson (Cambridge, England: Cambridge University Press, 1952), first ed. 1898.

2. Philalethes (Eirenaeus, seventeenth–century English hermetic writer). From the Hermetic Museum, Vol. II, A Short Vade Mecum to the Celestial Ruby (London: Vincent Stuart and John Watkins, 1953), p. 255.

3. Ramana Maharshi, Talks with Sri Ramana Maharshi 3 vols., ed. T. N. Venkatraman (Tiruvannamalai, South India, Venkatraman, 1955), p. 571.

4. Rumi, Divani Shamsi Tabriz, trans. R. A. Nicholson (Cambridge, England: Cambridge University Press, 1952), verse XLII.

5. Sri Sankaracharya, Upadeshasahasri II, A Thousand Teachings, trans. by Swami Jagadanada (Madras: Sri Ramakrishna math, 1949), p. XVI, p. 29.

6. Kirpal Singh, The Mystery of Death (Delhi: Ruhani Satsang, 1968), p. 92. Citing Hafiz.

7. Angelus Silesius, citing Cherubinischer Wandersmann (Paris: Aubier Editions Montaigne, n. d.), vol. IV, p. 101.

Sacred Writings

Acts of John (Apocryphal New Testament).
Translated by Montague Rhodes James. 1924-1953. London: Oxford
University Press.

Adi Granth (Sikh scripture).
Max Horten. 1924. *Die Philosophie des Islam*, Munich.

Anguttara-nikâya (Buddhist Pâli canon, part of the *Sutta-Pitaka*, or collection
of the Buddha's discourses).
W. Y. Evans-Wents. 1927-1951. *The Tibetan Book of the Dead*, London:
Oxford University Press.

Atharva-Veda (Hindu Vedic scripture).
Coomaraswamy: *Hinduism and Buddhism*,
idem: *Spiritual Authority and Temporal Power*.
Raghavan: *Indian Heritage*.

Bhagavad-Gîtâ (famous *sruti* teachings of Sri Krishna in the Hindu epic, the
Mahâbhârata, q.v.).
Translated by Swami Paramananda. 1942. *The Wisdom of China and
India*, edited by Lin Yutang. New York: Random House.

Bhagavatam, Srimad (Hindu scripture, life and teachings of Sri Krishna; one of
the main purânas).
Translated by Swami Prabhavananda. 1943. *The Wisdom of God.*
Hollywood, California: Vedanta Press, and New York, G. P. Putnam's Sons.

Bible (Judeo-Christian scripture).
The titles of the Books are to be found in the text; all passages are from the
King James Bible except where a 'D' indicates the Douay translation from
the Latin Vulgate; italicized page numbers indicate the New Testament.

Brahma-Sûtras (smriti commentary on the *Upanishads*, attributed to
Bâdarâyana, whom some identify with Vyâsa, q.v.).
Guènon. 1947. *L'Homme et son Devenir selon le Vèdânta*, Paris: Editions
Traditionnelles. 3rd ed.
Coomaraswamy. "Lîlâ," *Journal American Oriental Society*, Baltimore,
June, 1941.
Translated by Swami Vireswarananda. 1948. *Brahma-Sûtras*. Almora:
Advaita Ashrama.

Chândogya Upanishad (late Vedic scripture).
Translated by Robert Ernest Hume. 1921, 1931, 1934. *The Thirteen
Principal Upanishads.* London: Oxford University Press.

Translated by Richard C. Nicholson. 1945. Guénon: *Man and His Becoming*, London: Luzac.

Cloud of Unknowing, The (14th cent. English classic on contemplation. Edited by Dom Justin McCann. 1924-1943. *The Cloud of Unknowing.* London: Burns Oates and Washbourne.

Dhammapada (Buddhist Pali canon; famous utterances ascribed to the Buddha; part of the *Sutta-Pitaka*).
F. Max Müller. 1898. *The Sacred Books of the East*, Vol. X, Pt. I. Oxford: Clarendon Press.

Enoch, Book of (Old Testament Apocrypha).
Edited by R. H. Charles. 1913. *The Apocrypha and Pseudepigrapha of the Old Testament, in English.* Vol. II. Oxford: Clarendon Press.

Epistle of Discretion (14th cent. English spiritual treatise, presumably by the author of *The Cloud of Unknowing*, q.v.).
Edited by Dom Justin McCann. 1924–1943. *The Cloud of Unknowing, And other Treatises.* London: Burns Oates and Washbourne.

Epistle of Privy Counsel, The (14th cent. English spiritual treatise attributed to the author of *The Cloud of Unknowing*, q.v.).

Imitation of Christ, The (*De Imitatione Christi;* devotional classic, published anonymously in 1418; attributed to the German ecclesiastic and writer, Thomas a Kempis; 1380–1471).
Translation from the Latin published by Thomas Y. Crowell, New York, n. d.

Lankavatara Sutra (Mahâyâna Buddhist scripture originally in Sanskrit).

Mahâbhârata (great Hindu epic of the sage Vyâsa, q.v., which includes the *Bhagaval-Gîtâ*, q.v.).
B. G. Tilak. 1925. *The Arctic Home in the Vedas.* Poona City.

Maitri Upanishad (late Vedic scripture).
Translated by Robert Ernest Hume. 1921, 1931, 1934. *The Thirteen Principal Upanishads.* London: Oxford University Press.

Sefer Yetsirah ("Book of Creation"; Jewish esoterism; basic Kabbalistic text, along with *Zohar*, q.v.; probably written between 3rd and 6th century A.D., with teachings said to go back to Abraham).

Shepherd of Hermas, The (hortatory apocalyptic writing representing Apostolic Fathers in 3rd Christian generation, attributed to the brother of Pius I, Pope c. 139–154).
Coomaraswamy. 1942. "On Being in One's Right Mind," *The Review of Religion.* New York: Columbia University Press.

Shiva Samhitâ (Hindu Tantric treatise on hatha yoga and râja yoga).
Alain Daniélou. 1949. *Yoga, The Method of Re-Integration.* London: Christopher Johnson.

Sophic Hydrolith, The (or, Water Stone of the Wise; anonymous European alchemical text forming part of *The Hermetic Museum;* see under *All-Wise Doorkeeper).*

Suttanipâta (Buddhist Pâli canon, part of the *Sutta-Pitaka).*

Talmud (ancient body of Jewish civil and cononical law).
Leo Schaya. 1958. *L'Homme et l'Absolu selon la Kabbale.* Paris: Editions Buchet/Castel, Corrêa.

Tao Te Ching (the sacred book of the Taoists, left to the world by Lao-tse, c. 604–531 B.C., the great Chinese sage and founder of Taoism).
Translated by Ch'u Ta-Kao. 1937. London.

Tejo-bindu Upanishad (Vedic scripture; part of the *Krishna,* or Black, *Yajur-Veda,* dealing with yoga).
Alain Daniélou. 1949. *Yoga, the Method of Re-Integration.* London: Christopher Johnson.

Testament of Judah, The (Old Testament Apocrypha).

Theologia Germanica (famous 14th cent. German classic on the spiritual life, attributed to a priest of the Teutonic Order in Frankfort, c. 1350).

Tibetan Book of the Dead, The (the *Bardo Thödol,* "Liberation by Hearing on the After-Death Plane"; Mahâyâna Buddhist text, first committed to writing in 8th cent. A.D.; in general use throughout Tibet as a funeral ritual, and esoterically, as an initiatic support).
Translated by Lâma Kazi Dawa-Samdup, Edited by W. Y. Evans-Wentz. 1927–1951.*The Tibetan Book of the Dead.* Oxford University Press.

Tipitaka (the Three Divisions, or "Baskets," of Buddhist Pâli canon).

Yesod Hayirah ("The Foundation of Religious Fear"; author unknown, but work thought by Gollancz to be ultimately of the same origin as the *Shekel Hakodesh,* q.v.).
Translated by Hermann Gollancz. 1919. *Shekel Hakodesh* and *Yesod Hayirah.* London: Oxford University Press.

Yoga Darshana (comprises the Yoga Sutras of Patanjali, q.v. and the Commentary of Vyâsa, q.v.).
Alain Daniélou. 1949. *Yoga, the Method of Re-Integration.* London: Christopher Johnson.

Yoga-Vasishtha (Hindu antiquity: teachings of the sage Vasishtha to Prince Râma, transcribed 3rd cent. B.C. by Vâlmiki, q.v. under *Râmâyana*).
Translated from the Sanskrit by Hari Prasad Shastri. 1937, 1946, 1952. *The World Within the Mind.* London: Shanti Sadan.

Zendavesta, The (Zoroastrian scripture).
Translated by James Darmsteter. 1883. *Ormazd Yast.* Edited by F. Max Müller. *The Sacred Books of the East.* Oxford: Clarendon Press.

Zohar (Sefer Ha-Zohar, "Book of Splendour"; Jewish Kabbalistic book introduced into Spain by Moses de Leon, q.v., in 13th cent.; attributed by him to Simeon ben Yohai, 2nd cent. A.D.).

Spiritual Leaders

'Abd al-'Aziz b. Sulaymân (Abû al-Rasibi; d. 767; Sufi ascetic and devotee,
contemporary with Râbi'a of Bastra, q.v.).
Margaret Smith. 1928. *Râbi'a the Mystic & Her Fellow-Saints in Islâm.*
London: Cambridge University Press.

'Abd al-Qâdir al-Jîlânî (1078–1166; great Persian Sufi of Baghdad, founded
Qâdirîyah Order, the first large Sufic order; tremendous popular devotion).
Margaret Smith. 1950. *Readings from the Mystics of Islâm.* London:
Luzac.

Abû Hurayrah (one of the Companions of the Prophet Muhammad; many of
the more esoteric ahâdîth were transmitted by him).
Abû Bakr Sirâj ad-Din. 1956. "The Origins of Sufism," *Islamic Quarterly,*
April 1956.

Abulafia, Abraham (b. Saragossa 1240; eminent Spanish Jewish Kabbalist).
Gershom G. Scholem. 1954. *Major Trends in Jewish Mysticism.* New York:
Schocken Books.

Abu 'l-Qâsim al-'Irâqî (13th cent. Islamic alchemist).
Paul Geuthner. 1923. *Kitâb al-'Ilm al-Muktasab fî Zirâ'at adh-Dhahab*
(Book of Knowledge Acquired Concerning the Cultivation of Gold);
Translated from the Arabic by E. J. Holmyard. Paris.

Abû Sa'îd ibn Abi 'l-Khayr (967–1049; Persian Sufi master, noted for miraculous
life, character insight).
E. G. Browne. 1902. *Literary History of Persia.* London.

Ahmad al-'Alawî, Shaykh (Abu ';-'Abbâs Ahmad ibn Mustafa 'l-'Alawî; 1869-
1934; famous Algerian spiritual pole (qutb); founder 'Alawîyah branch of
Shâdhilîyah Order).
Cited by M. Lings. 1960. *Folkways Records Album* No. FR 8943, 1960.

Akka Mahâdêvî (12th cent. A.D. Vîrasaiva Hindu woman saint).
Edited and published by The Ramakrishna Vedanta Centre. 1955. *Women
Saints of East and West,* London.

Alphidius (alchemical author cited in *The Glory of the World,* q.v.).

Ambrose, Saint (340?–397; bishop of Milan, Church Father, baptized Saint
Augustine).
cited by Saint Thomas Aquinas: *Summa Theol.,* I-II, 109.I.

Angelus Silesius (real name Johannes Scheffler, 1624-1677; German
theosophist school of Boehme, q.v., and poet; as priest became coadjutor
to the prince bishop of Breslau).

Translated by Henri Plard. 1946. *Cherubinischer Wandersmann*, VI. 50; from *Angelus Silesius, Pèlerin chèrubinique.* Paris: Aubier.

Ansârî ('Abdullâh, d. 1088; Persian Sufi master and poet).
Translated by Sardar Sir Jogendra Singh. 1939. *The Persian Mystics, The Invocations of Sheikh 'Abdullâh Ansârî of Herat.* London: John Murray.

Aquinas, Saint Thomas (1225?–1274; Italian scholastic, philosopher, called Angelic Doctor, Prince of Scholastics; known for systematizing Catholic theology).
Edited by Anton C. Pegis. 1945. *Summa Theologica*, I. 91. 2; *Basic Writings of Saint Thomas Aquinas.* New York: Random House.

'Attâr (Farîd al-Dîn; d. 1229; eminent Persian mystic poet and Sufi biographer).
Smith. *Jawhar al-Dhât, Kulliyât; Mystics of Islâm*, no. 91.

Augustine, Saint (Aurelius Augustinus, 354–430; Church Father and Doctor; renowned philosopher and theologian; bishop of Hippo).

Baal Shem, Israel (d. 1760; founder of modern Hasidism in Poland).
Cited in Schuon. 1953. *Perspectives spirituelles et Faits humains.* Paris: Cahiers du Sud.
Gershom G. Scholem. 1954. *Major Trends in Jewish Mysticism.* New York: Schocken Books.

Basil, Saint (the Great; 330?–379; older brother of Gregory of Nyssa, q.v., Doctor of the Church, bishop of Caesarea, known as founder of monastic institutions).
Cited in Coomaraswamy. 1946. *De Sanctu Spiritu*, c. 18; *Figures of Speech or Figures of Thought*, London: Luzac.
Schuon. 1950. *L'Oeil du Coeur.* Paris: Gallimard.

Bâyazîd al-Bistâmî (Abû Yazîd Tayfûr b. 'Isâ al-Bistâmî; d. 875; great Persian Sufic authority, first of "intoxicated" Sufis).

Bernard, Saint (1091–1153; French Doctor of the Church, known as Thaumaturgus of the West; founder Cistercian monastery of Clairvaux, preached Second Crusade).

Boehme, Jacob (1575–1624; Christian gnosis; leading German theosophist).

Bonaventura, Saint (Giovanni di Fidanza, 1221–1274; Italian Scholastic philosopher, cardinal, eminent medieval writer and contemplative, "the Seraphic Doctor").

Brahmânanda, Swâmi (1863–1922; disciple and transmitter of teachings of Sri Ramakrishna, q.v.).
Translated by Odette de Saussure and Jean Herbert. 1945. *Discipline*

monastique, Paris: Maisonneuve, and Neuchatel, Delachaux et Niestlé.
Vol. I, 2nd ed.

Catherine of Siena, Saint (1347–1380; Dominican Tertiary, renowned for
revelations; adviser to rulers of Church and State, one of the great
intellectual women of the Church).

Chaitanya (1486–1534; great Vaishnava saint of India).
Sir Jadunath Sarkar. 1932. *Chaitanya's Life and Teachings,* Calcutta

Chih-k'ai (fl. A.D. 575; Chinese Buddhist founder of the Tendai doctrine which
later formed a school of Japanese Buddhism).
Shumjô; Translated by Harper Havelock Coates and Ryugaku Ishizuka.
1949. *Hônen the Buddhist Saint.* Kyoto.

Chuang-tse (d. c. 275 B.C.; leading exponent of Taoism; his teachings
contained in the *Nan-Hua-Chên-Ching* of thirty-three chapters).
Translated from Chinese by Herbert A. Giles. 1889. *Chuang Tzu, Mystic,
Moralist, and Social Reformer.* London: Quaritch.
Translated by Lin Yutang based on Giles. Edited by Lin Yutang. 1942. *The
Wisdom of China and India.* New York: Random House.
French translation by Léon Wieger. 1950. *Les Pères du Système taoiste.*
Paris: Cathasia.

Cordovero, Moses ben Jacob (1552–1570; Spanish Kabbalist at Safed, in Upper
Galilee, authority on *Zohar,* q.v.).
Gershom G. Scholem. 1954. *Major trends in Jewish Mysticism.* New York:
Schocken Books, 3rd ed.

Dante (Alighieri: 1265–1321; Italy's foremost Christian poet).

Dionysius (the Areopagite; traditionally accepted as the Athenian of the 1st
cent. converted by Saint Paul *Acts,* XVII. 34; link between Platonism and
Christianity, pole of Christian gnosis).
Translated by C. E. Rolt. 1920–1940. *Dionysius the Areopagite, On the
Divine Names, and the Mystical Theology.* London: Society for Promoting
Christian Knowledge.

Dôgen (Zenji; 1200–1253; founder Sôtô branch of Zen Buddhism in Japan).
Reikichi Kita and Kiichi Nagaya. *Fukan Zazengi.* Translated Ruth F.
Sasaki. *How Altruism Is Cultivated in Zen.*
Translated by Harper Havelock Coates and Ryugaku Ishizuka. 1949.
Shôbôgenzô; Hônen the Buddhist Saint. Kyoto.

Eckhart (Johannes, known as Meister Eckhart; 1260?–?1327; German
Dominican theologian, and foremost of the Rhenish contemplatives
renowned for Christian gnosis; Coomaraswamy says of Eckhart that he

resumes and concentrates "in one consistent demonstration the spiritual being of Europe at its highest tension"—*The Transformation of Nature in Art,* Harvard Univ. Press, 1935, p. 61).

Franz Pfeiffer. 1857. *Meister Eckhart.* Leipzig. Translated by C. de B. Evans. 1924. London: John M. Watkins.

Raymond Bernard Blakney. 1941. *Meister Eckhart: A Modern Translation.* New York: Harper & Brothers.

Ezra (Hebrew priest, 5th cent. B.C.).
Gershom G. Scholem. 1954. *Major Trends in Jewish Mysticism.* New York: Schocken Books. 3rd ed.

Ficino, Marsilio (1433–1499; eminent Italian philosopher, writer, and Renaissance Platonist).
Paul Oskar Kristeller, Translated by Virginia Conant. 1943. *The Philosophy of Marsilio Ficino.* New York: Columbia University Press.

Francis of Assisi, Saint (Giovanni Francesco Bernardone; 1182–1226; Italian monk, preacher, founder of Franciscans; renowned mediaeval Christian saint).
Translated by Thomas Okey. 1910–1944. *The Little Flowers of Saint Francis.* New York: Everyman's Library.

Francis de Sales, Saint (1567–1622; Savoyard nobleman, bishop of Geneva, Doctor of the Church; collaborated with Saint Jeanne de Chantal in founding Order of the Visitation of Our Lady).

Al-Ghazâlî (Abû Hâmid; d. 1111; famous Muslim theologian, Sufi authority, from Khurâsân).
Margaret Smith. 1950. *Readings from the Mystics of Islâm.* ("The Revivification of Religion"). London: Luzac.

Ghost Dancers at Wounded Knee, The (South Dakota, scene of the infamous massacre of Sioux in 1890).
As rendered by René Thévenin and Paul Coze. 1952. *Moeurs et Histoire des Peaux-Rouges.* Paris: Payot.

Gujarati Hymn (Hinduism).
Cited in C. F. Andrews. 1929. *Mahatma Gandhi's Ideas.* London: Allen & Unwin.

Hâfiz (Shams al-Dî; d. 1389; Persian Sufi master and mystical poet, famous for his *Dîwân*).
Margaret Smith. 1950. *Dîwân; Readings from the Mystics of Islâm.* London: Luzac.

Hakuim (1683–1768; renovator of Japanese Rinzai school of Zen, and
outstanding figure of later Zen period).
Translated by R. D. M. Shaw. 1963. *The Embossed Tea Kettle and Other
Works of Hakuin Zenjii.* London: Allen & Unwin.
D. T. Suzuki. 1949, 1958. *Essays in Zen Buddhism* (First Series). London:
Rider.

Hermes (Trismegistus, "Thrice-Greatest"; the sacerdotal wisdom of Egyptian
antiquity).
Edited and Translated from the Greek and the Latin by Walter Scott.
1924–1936. *Hermetica.* Oxford: Clarendon Press.

Hildegard, Saint (Hildegard von Bingen; 1098–1179; famous German
contemplative in the tradition of Christian gnosis).
Olten. 1957. *Geheimnis der Liebe* (The Mystery of Love). Switzerland:
Walter-Verlag.

Huang Po (d. c. A.D. 850; Chinese Zen, or Dhyâna, Buddhist master).
Recorded by P'ei Hsiu of the T'and Dynasty, Translated by John Blofedl.
1958. *The Zen Teaching of Huang Po.* London: Rider.

Hujwîrî ('Alî b. 'Uthmân al-Jullâbî al-Hujwîrî; d. c. 1070; celebrated Sufi
anthologist, orig. of Afghanistan).
Hujwîrî, Translated from the Persian by R. A. Nicholson. 1911, 1936, 1959.
Ksshf al-Mahjûb. London: Luzac.

Ibn 'Arabî (Muhyî al-Dîn ibn al-'Arabî; 1165–1240; from Murcia, Spain; died in
Damascus; renowned pole of Sufi metaphysic).

Ibn al-'Arîf (d. 1141; Andalusian Sufic master, famed for science of virtues).
Translated from Arabic into Spanish by Miguel Asin Palacios, and from
Spanish into French by F. Cavallera. 1933. *Mahâsin al-Majâlis* ("The
Virtues of the Sessions"). Paris: Paul Geuthner.

Ibn al-Fârid (Sharafu'ddîn "Umar; 1181–1235; of Cairo;" greatest of Arab
mystical poets).

Jâmî (Nûr al-Dîn 'Abd al-Rahmân; d. 1492; famous Afghan Sufi philosopher,
poet).
Translated by E. H. Whinfield and Mîrzâ Muhammad Kazvînî. 1906–1928.
Lawâ'ih ('Flashes of Light'). London: Royal Asiatic Society.

Jîlî ('Abd al-Karîm; 1366–1428; great Sufic metaphysician, taught in Baghdad).
R. A. Nicholson. 1921. *Studies in Islamic Mysticism.* London: Cambridge
University Press.
Titus Burckhardt. 1953. *De l'Homme universel.* Lyon: P. Derain.

Junayd (Abu'l-Qâsim al-Junayd; d. 910; famous Sufi of Persian extraction, taught at Baghdad).

Kabîr (1450?–1518; spiritual leader and mystic poet of Benares whose teachings are revered by Hindus and Muslims alike).

Law, William (1686–1761; English divine, and mystical writer, school of Boehme, q.v.; after Cambridge Platonists, most eminent of English contemplatives).
Edited by Stephen Hobhouse. 1938–1949. *Selected Mystical Writings of William Law.* London: Rockliff.

Liguori, Saint Alphonsus (1696–1787; Italian prelate, founded Redemptorist Order; bishop of Sant' Agata dei Goti; Doctor of the Church; known for theological treatises and other writings).
Translated from the Italian by the Benecdictine Convent of Perpetual Adoration. 1935. *Conformity to the Will of God.* 7th ed. Clyde, Missouri.

Maharshi, Sri Ramana (1879–1950; Hindu sage, noted for method of intellectual penetration).

Matilda of Magdeburg (1210–1297; a foremost German contemplative in the realm of Christian gnosis).
Translated by Lucy Menzies. 1953. *The Revelations of Mechthild of Magdeburg,* or *The Flowing Light of the Godhead.* London: Longmans, Green.

Milarepa (Jetsün-Milarepa; 1052?–1135; famous Tibetan saint, one of the great gurus of the Kargyütpa School of Northern Buddhism).
Translated by Lâma Kazi Dawa-Samdup, Edited by W. Y. Evans-Wentz. 1928. *Tibet's Great Yogi Milarepa, a Biography from the Tibetan, being the Jetsön-Kahbum.* London: Oxford University Press.

Mîrâ Bâî (1504?–1550; princess and Hindu saint of Northern India, famed for her devotional poetry).
C. F. Andrews. 1929. *Mahatma Gandhi's Ideas.* London: Allen & Unwin.

Moyi, Ananda (contemporary Hindu woman saint).
Translated into French by Jean Herbert (from an English translation by H. R. Joshi called *Sat-Bani.* Calcutta: Chuckervetty, Chatterjee). 1943. *Aux Sources de la Joie.* Paris & Neuchatel: Editions Ophrys.

Nâgârjuna (fl. 2nd cent. A.D.; thirteenth or fourteenth Buddhist Patriarch, founder of Mahâyâna school of Northern Buddhism).
W. Y. Evans-Wentz. 1954. *The Tibetan Book of the Great Liberation.*

London: Oxford University Press.

Mircea Eliade. 1954. *Le Yoga, Immortalité*. Paris: Payot.

Philo (Judaeus; fl. late 1st cent. B.C. and early 1st cent. A.D.; famous Hellenistic-Jewish philosopher of Alexandria, "the Jewish Plato", sought to harmonize Greek and Platonic philosophy with the Pentateuch).
Ananda K. Coomaraswamy. 1947. *Time and Eternity*. Ascona, Switzerland: Artibus Asiae.

Plotinus (A.D. 205?–270; Roman, b. in Egypt, studied at Alexandria under Ammonius Saccas; the great exponent of Neoplatonish).
Translated by Stephen MacKenna. 1956 (1st publ. 1917–1930). *The Enneads*. London: Faber & Faber.
Grace H. Turnbull. 1934. *The Essence of Plotinus*. New York: Oxford University Press.

Rûmî (Jalâl al-Dîn; 1207–1273; of Balkh, later to Konia in Asia Minor; founder of Mevlevi Order of dervishes, and Persia's greatest Sufi poet; see also *Dîvâni Shamsi Tabriz*).

Ruysbroeck, Jan van (1293–1381; leading Flemish mystical theologian, called "the Ecstatic Doctor").

Sai Baba (1856–1918; contemporary Indian saint much venerated by both Hindus and Muslims, noted for miraculous life).
Arthur Osborne. 1957. *The Incredible Sai Baba*. London: Rider. (Calcutta: Orient Longmans.)

Sankarâchârya, Sri (fl. A.D. 800; Hindu metaphysician, leading exponent of *Advaita-Vedânta*, the doctrine of non-duality).

Sânti-deya (7th cent. follower of Nâgâjuna's, q.v., Mâdhyamika school of Mahâyâna Buddhism, and a guru in the succession of the Nâlandâ Buddhist university and monastery in Bihâr, India).
Translated from the Sanskrit by L. D. Barnett. 1909, 1947. *The Path of Light*, being the *Bodhi-charyâvatâra* and to which is appended the *Sikshâsamuchchaya*. London: John Murray.

Seng-ts'an (c. A.D. 600; 3rd Patriarch in Dhyana school of Chinese Buddhism).
D. T. Suzuki. 1950. *Manual of Zen Buddhism*. London: Rider.

Shabistarî (Sa'd al-Dîn Mahmûd; d. 1320; one of the greatest Persian Sufi poets).
Translated by Florence Lederer. n.d. *The Secret Rose Garden of Sa'd Ud Din Mahmud Shabistari*. Lahore: Ashraf Publication.

Shiblî (Abû Bakr Dulaf bl Jahdar al-Shiblî; d. c. 945–6 A.D.; famous Sufi of Baghdad, disciple of Junayd, q.v.).

Translated by R. A. Nicholson. 1911–1959. *Kashf al-Mahjûb*. London: Luzac.

Sivananda, Swani (Sarasvati; 1887–1963; contemporary Hindu, exponent of *Japa* and authority on meditation techniques).
Translated by Charles Andrieu and Jean Herbert. 1950. *La Pratique de la Méditation* (from *Concentration and Meditation*, 1945, which was not obtainable). Paris: Albin Michel.
Rishikesh. 1952. *Japa Yoga*. India: The Yoga-Vedanta Forest University.

Sterry, Peter (1613–1672; one of the leading Cambridge Platonists).
Vivian de Sola Pinto. 1934. *Peter Sterry, Platonist and Puritan*. London: Cambridge University Press.

Suhrawardî (Shihâb al=Dîn Suhrawardî Halabî al-Maqtûl; Sufi philosopher at Aleppo famed for his *Hikmatu 'l-Ishrâq*, "Philosophy of Illumination"; put to death in A.D. 1191 on charges of heresy by a son of Saladin).
M. Horten. 1912. *Die Philosophie der Erleuchtung nach Suhrawardi*. Halle a. S.

Suso, Henry (real name Heinrich von Berg; 1300?–1366; one of the foremost German contemplatives, follower of Eckhart).
Translated by James M. Clark. 1953. *The Little Book of Eternal Wisdom*. London: Faber & Faber.

Tauler (Johannes; 1300?–1361; famous Rhenish Dominican contemplative, school of Eckhart; called "the Illuminated Doctor").
Translated by Susanna Winkworth. 1858. *Life and Sermons of Dr. John Tauler*. New York.

Teresa of Avila, Saint (1515–1582; Spanish mystical saint, co-founder with Saint John of the Cross, q.v., of the Order of Discalced Carmelites).

Traherne, Thomas (1637?–1674; English contemplative poet, religious writer, chaplain, Platonist).
Edited by Bertram Dobell. 1908–1958. *Centuries of Meditations*. London: P. J. and A. E. Dobell.

Tulsi Dâs (1532–1623; considered greatest poet of medieval Hindustan; devotee of Râma, wrote a version in Awadhi of the *Râmâyana*, q.v., called *Râmcharit-mânas*).
Translated by Swami Nikhilananda. 1942. *The Gospel of Sri Ramakrishna*. New York: Ramakrishna-Vivekananda Center.
Swami Sivananda. 1952. *Japa Yoga*. Rishikesh, India.

Vivekananda, Swami (1863–1902; celebrated disciple of Sri Ramakrishna, whose teachings he drastically compromised through unassimilated confrontation with Western civilization).

Vyâsa (Hindu sage, Vedic period; compiler of Vedas, author of the *Mahâbhârata*, q.v.).
   Sir Jadunath Sarkar. 1932. *Chaitanya's Life and Teachings.* Calcutta.

Yoka Daishi (d. A.D. 713; Chinese Zen master, disciple of Hui-nêng, q.v.).
   D. T. Suzuki. 1950. *Manual of Zen Buddhism.* London: Rider.

Communing with the Spirit of Your Unborn Child
by Dawson Chruch

"Wow! This book is incredible! An amazing book, a beautiful theme, well written & produced!"
—*Ken Carey, The Starseed Transmissions*

This "excellent" book, "an outstanding addition to prenatal literature" (Midwifery Today), is a clear how-to manual for parents exploring pregnancy, birth and infancy from a spiritual perspective.

Using photographs, diagrams and meditations, this powerful, inspirational classic outlines in simple, practical language a step-by-step approach that enables parents to communicate with the inner magic of the unborn child.

Available as a book or audio tape.
Also sold as a set.

Intuition Workout by Nancy Rosanoff

This practical training manual teaches simple techniques to access our deepest sources of inner knowing in any situation.

The author, one of America's outstanding corporate trainers, shows that intuition, like a muscle, is strengthened by training. She outlines dozens of case histories and step-by-step exercises proven effective even with "non-intuitive" people.

"A workout in cultivating our inner resources and building self-confidence. Once you know how to do it, you can adapt the techniques to any situation."
—*New York Daily News*

Available as a book or audio tape.
Also sold as a set.

Meditation For Children by Deborah Rozman

This is a new updated edition of the bestselling classic on growing a close, nurturing family. These simple methods teach children to relate to life with new confidence and joy.

"...successfully integrated yoga, concentration, meditation, creative fantasy, movement, psychology and —most assuredly—love in a way that clearly shows interested adults a path to fulfilling children's spiritual needs...many positive side effects occur...a heightening sense of community, a sense of trust between adult and child, an ability to focus energy, greater creativity and a calm confidence."
—*New Age Journal*

The Heart of the Healer
Edited by Dawson Church & Dr. Alan Sherr

A collection of outstanding figures on the leading edge of conventional and holistic medicine, including Bernie Siegel, Norman Cousins and Prince Charles, draw on their deepest personal experiences to explore how we get in touch with the essence of wellness. This classic has been called "Exceptional" —*SSC Booknews;* "Thought-provoking" —*Publisher's Weekly;* "Profound...provocative" —*Ram Dass.*

Voice Power
by Dr. Joan Kenley

The sound of your voice can have more than five times the impact of the words you say. *Voice Power* shows you how to draw on the resources of your whole body to release your natural voice—the voice that is truly and fully you. It shows you how to integrate the deepest roots of your personality, your vitality and your sexuality, to project charisma and confidence.

   "...a fun read as well as a very practical, thorough book."   —*Network Magazine*

Finding the Great Creative You
by Lynne Garnett, Ph.D.

This is the career book of the 1990's, focusing not on "getting a job," but on maximizing creativity and personal fulfillment. It is powerful in its ability to tap into the courage inherent in each of us that allows us to discover our deepest visions and live them fully. It moves us beyond "just getting by" and "making a living" to unlock the power and passion each of us needs to make our life abundant, joyful, and productive.

   "...worth taking more than a minute to read."
   –*Ken Blanchard, co-author, The One Minute Manager*

The Unmanifest Self
by Ligia Dantes

This book, like a warm, gentle friend, guides us toward an experience of self-transformation that is quite different from our usual waking consciousness, that is vastly more than an improved version of the old self. *The Unmanifest Self* teaches us the art of *objective self-observation*, a powerful tool to separate the essential truth of who we are from the labyrinth of thoughts and emotions in which we are often caught.

   "...beautiful and inspiring."   —*Willis Harmon*

Order Form

Date _____

Name _____

Address _____

City _____ State _____ Zip _____

Phone _____

Please send a catalog to my friend:

Name _____

Address _____

City _____ State _____ Zip _____

Quantity Discounts!

$2 off the second item
$3 off the third item
$4 off the forth item, etc...

Item	Qty.	Price	Amount
Communing With the Spirit of Your Unborn Child (book)		$8.95	
Communing With the Spirit of Your Unborn Child (tape)		$9.95	
Intuition Workout (book)		$9.95	
Intuition Workout (tape)		$9.95	
Meditation for Children		$9.95	
The Heart of the Healer		$14.95	
Voice Power (hardback book)		$18.95	
Finding the Great Creative You		$10.95	
The Unmanifest Self		$9.95	
Love is a Secret		$9.95	

Subtotal	
Quantity Discount	
Calif. res. add 6.5% sales tax	
Shipping	
Grand Total	

Add for shipping:
Bookrate: $2.00 for the first item, $1.00 for ea. add. item
First Class/UPS: $4.00 for first item, $2.00 ea. add. item
Foreign: Double shipping rates

Check type of payment:

☐ Check or money order enclosed

☐ VISA   ☐ MasterCard

Acct. # _____

Exp. Date _____

Signature _____

Send order to:

**Aslan Publishing
310 Blue Ridge Drive
Boulder Creek, CA 95006**

or call to order:

**(408) 338-7504
(800) 372-3100 US or
(800) 423-5784 in California**

Order Form

(Please print legibly)   Date _____

Name _____

Address _____

City _____ State _____ Zip _____

Phone _____

Please send a catalog to my friend:

Name _____

Address _____

City _____ State _____ Zip _____

Quantity Discounts!
$2 off the second item
$3 off the third item
$4 off the forth item, etc...

Item	Qty.	Price	Amount
Communing With the Spirit of Your Unborn Child (book)		$8.95	
Communing With the Spirit of Your Unborn Child (tape)		$9.95	
Intuition Workout (book)		$9.95	
Intuition Workout (tape)		$9.95	
Meditation for Children		$9.95	
The Heart of the Healer		$14.95	
Voice Power (hardback book)		$18.95	
Finding the Great Creative You		$10.95	
The Unmanifest Self		$9.95	
Love is a Secret		$9.95	

Subtotal	
Quantity Discount	
Calif. res. add 6.5% sales tax	
Shipping	
Grand Total	

Add for shipping:
Bookrate: $2.00 for the first item, $1.00 for ea. add. item
First Class/UPS: $4.00 for first item, $2.00 ea. add. item
Foreign: Double shipping rates

Check type of payment:

☐ Check or money order enclosed

☐ VISA   ☐ MasterCard

Acct. # _____

Exp. Date _____

Signature _____

Send order to:

**Aslan Publishing
310 Blue Ridge Drive
Boulder Creek, CA 95006**

or call to order:

**(408) 338-7504
(800) 372-3100 US or
(800) 423-5784 in California**